Signs,
Symbols,
and
Solutions

Arnold P. Goldstein

Donald W. Kodluboy

Research Press   2612 North Mattis Avenue   Champaign, Illinois 61822
(800) 519-2707   www.researchpress.com

Contents

Figures & Tables

FIGURES

TABLES

Youth Gangs in the United States

This introduction sets the stage for our subsequent in-depth consideration of gangs in schools by describing the history and current status of youth gangs in the United States. What constitutes a gang—on its face not a difficult question—has proven over the decades a formidable definitional challenge. We believe that many of the definitions proposed are correct, though they differ from one another, because there have been and still are many different types of youth groups legitimately categorized as gangs. Following our clarification of this definitional confusion and establishment of the wide range of groups appropriately called gangs, we next focus on the current youth gang situation in the United States. Though unfortunately no U.S. government agency regularly tracks the incidence and behavior of youth gangs in this country, a number of independent surveys, which we will describe, have reported useful information about numbers of gangs and gang members, age range, gender distribution, migration causes and patterns, and other valuable demographic matters.

As prelude to our examination of effective gang intervention programs, we also in the present chapter describe the primary gang intervention strategies in the United States, both past and present. Detached worker programs, the opportunities provision era, the emergence and current dominance of criminal justice strategies, and our belief in a new orientation—comprehensive programming—will each be described. Much of this evolution of intervention strategies took place before youth gangs surfaced in school settings. This benign circumstance unfortunately no longer prevails, and thus we will complete the present chapter by outlining how a comprehensive gang intervention strategy might optimally be framed and concretized for the management, reduction, and even elimination of gang presence and influence in the school environment.

DEFINITION

If someone were to ask 1,000 teachers or other citizens to define the term *school,* most of those responding likely would agree on a few core aspects and differ in numerous other ways. School, they might concur, is a place with teachers and students, the former trying to impart knowledge to the latter. Beyond that, respondents would envision that place as large or small, public or private, successful in its mission or not, well-kept or run-down. The important point is that since schools are indeed all of the above, all definitions are correct for some schools, and none is correct for all.

A similar pattern can be discerned in the efforts of criminologists, sociologists, educators, and others to define *gang.* Almost all would agree that a gang is a visible group of youths who engage at least some of the time in behaviors that are troublesome to the community of which they are a part—and sometimes are illegal. Beyond this, the dozen prominent definitions of *gang* that have emerged during this century (see Goldstein, 1991) vary in such descriptive features as number and age of group participants, level and nature of organizational structure and leadership, illegality of typical behaviors, community (citizen and police) response, and more. As is the case for schools, all of these varying qualities describe some youth gangs, but none describes all. Let us look at two specific examples. Table 1 presents the key features of gangs according to Miller (1974) and as seen by the New York State Task Force on Juvenile Gangs (Dunston, 1990).

Table 1 in a sense defines the end points of a continuum of definitions of *gang,* all of which are partly accurate. Some gangs last 30 years; others endure for but 30 days. For some gangs, membership is largely a small, fixed set of individuals living and hanging out together for many hours every day. For others, much of the membership comes and goes, are "gang" some of the time yet not others. One member of the New York State task force (Dunston, 1990) described many New York City gangs as akin to pick-up basketball games—involving these ten youths today, perhaps five of them and five new youths the next. For some gangs, membership is intergenerational: grandfather, father, and the youth of today. For others, it is ephemeral. As Klein, Maxson, and Cunningham (1991) note:

> Street gangs are said to be well-suited to drug distribution because of their internal structure, which is hierarchical and highly controlled. In fact, however, street gangs are normally loosely structured and ill-controlled. Turnover is heavy and relatively constant, so that experienced members wax and wane in their participation, while older members

Table 1—Contrasting Definitions of "Gang"

1974	1991
Structured organization	Loose organization
Stable leadership	Changeable leadership
Territorial identification	Criminal activity–oriented
Continuous association	Irregular association
Specific purposes	Amorphous purposes
Illegal activity	Illegal and legal activity

are rapidly replaced by new recruits. Only in *West Side Story* is control wielded effectively by the few: in real street gangs, multiple cliques, dyads, and triads are the common units of companionship, each responsive to its own age peers rather than to powerful (or older) leaders. For drug distributors, such a haphazard organizational structure does not provide the basis for an effective distributional system. (p. 627)

Most U.S. youth gangs fall somewhere between these two organizational extremes. The problem of defining *gang*, however, grows not only from the tremendous variety of membership, structural, leadership, and behavioral characteristics, but also from the numerous terms that have been employed to describe shades of difference among such youth groups. Table 2 presents a list of definitional distinctions, drawn primarily from that suggested by Spergel and Curry (1993).

Combine the many definitions of *gang*, the diverse features present or absent from these definitions, and the wide variety of ganglike groups that have been identified, and it is little wonder that school personnel and community figures have so much difficulty answering the seemingly simple, but in reality quite challenging, question: Do we have a gang here? Chapter 2 of this book, "Signs and Symbols," and Chapter 3, "Becoming a Gang Member," each provide a wealth of information to enhance the reader's ability to answer this question when it arises.

GANG DEMOGRAPHICS

The National Youth Gang Center surveyed 2,007 law enforcement agencies in 1995, inquiring into the presence of gang activity in these jurisdictions. Results of this national effort revealed the presence of 23,388 gangs and 664,906 gang members (U.S. Office of Juvenile

Table 2—Definitional Distinctions

Gang
A group of persons with a common identity who interact on a regular basis and whose activities the community views as intolerable, illegitimate, criminal, or a combination thereof.

Street gang
A group of persons engaged in a wide variety of significant illegitimate or criminal activity. Emphasis in this definition is on location.

Posse/crew
More than the traditional gang, this group of persons is committed to criminal activity for economic gain, particularly drug trafficking. May be loosely organized and/or connected to an adult criminal organization.

Copycat gang
A group of persons who identify with and emulate the behaviors and mannerisms of urban gang members. These groups are ephemeral, commit minor acts of delinquency, and have little actual contact with functioning gangs.

Pretend gang
Elementary age youth who, as a play activity, engage as a group in ganglike behaviors.

Table 2—Definitional Distinctions CONTINUED

Clique or set	A small subgroup of a larger gang. The clique may be a cohesive subset of perhaps two to five gang youths; the set is an entire same-aged faction of a larger gang (e.g., the Ancients, the Seniors, the Juniors, the Pee Wees).
Delinquent group	A less-organized, more transient group of juveniles whose law-violating behavior is less serious, violent, or persistent than that displayed by gang members.
Criminal organization	A well-organized, stable, and sophisticated group committed to income-producing criminal activity. Members are essentially employees who may make frequent use of intimidation and violence.
Street group	A group of persons coalescing primarily around formally or informally organized social or athletic activities.
Prosocial gang	A youth gang previously engaging in illegitimate or illegal behavior, now committed to and engaging in constructive business, social, and/or community activities.

Justice and Delinquency Prevention, 1995). A major national survey conducted by Klein (1995), inquiring skillfully into the gang situations in 800 cities and towns in the United States, yielded an estimate of 9,000 youth gangs and 400,000 gang members. While exact figures are not obtainable, these latter estimates are, based on the manner in which they were derived, the soundest approximations available. A U.S. Department of Justice (1991) survey of over 20 million school-children found that over 3 million of them (15%) reported a gang presence in their schools. Youth gangs in this country are widely dis-tributed geographically, and though still concentrated in Los Angeles, Chicago, and a few other areas, almost no state is spared. Figure 1, reflecting Klein's (1995) effort, displays just how widely distributed gangs are.

Note that we said gangs are distributed, not spread. The term *spread* implies origination in one location, followed by movement toward another. While some gang spread ("franchising," "hiving off") occurs, particularly from one city to another along the interstate highway system, as in a spread of drug trafficking, most such gang migration is no migration at all. Gangs in most of the 800 cities in which they have appeared originated de novo in those cities. Films, television, and other media teach all it is necessary to know in order to initiate one's own gang, precluding the need for outsiders to come in and set up shop. Furthermore, most of the gang migration that does take place results from family decisions to move, often to escape gang influence and involvement! Subsequently, the youths being "protected" start their own gangs in the new locations.

Males outnumber female gang members approximately 15 to 1 (Klein, 1995). While some girl gangs are still essentially auxiliaries to corresponding boy gangs—and still function in such auxiliary roles as sexual partners, drug and weapons carriers, and the like—the number of independent female gangs has grown steadily in recent decades. Females generally join gangs later than do males, leave earlier, and are less likely to graduate to adult criminal careers.

Figure 1—Gang Distribution in the U.S.

Note. From *The American Street Gang* (p. 95) by M.W. Klein, 1995. Copyright © 1995 by Oxford University Press, Inc. Used by permission of Oxford University Press, Inc.

However, while they are members they can be and are every bit as violent as seriously violent male gang members.

Up until the early 1970s, almost all U.S. youth gangs had a primarily territorial focus. Their main purpose was to claim and protect their neighborhood turf. Violence served to maintain their territorial identity and to express group solidarity. Around this time, low-level gang involvement in drug trafficking began. The drug business in this country is sufficiently lucrative that it has been, and remains, primarily the business of organized adult crime. For this reason, and as a result of the typically loose organization of most youth gangs, adolescents have usually been involved in the drug business in the more dangerous and less financially rewarding capacities of street seller, runner, lookout, and the like. Most youth gangs are still territorial collectives. In spite of media depiction and police assertion to the contrary, the large majority of adolescent gangs are *not* involved—even at the low levels just described—in the drug business. It is important to note, however, that in some cities a close linkage exists between gangs and drugs. Gangs that are more entrepreneurially oriented in this manner are more violent, more lethally armed, and more of a potentially serious threat to safety and security in schools as well as in other settings. We will have more to say about gang violence in chapter 5.

While increased involvement in drug trafficking is the case for only a minority of youth gang members, or for rather more gang members in select cities, other changes in gang behavior in recent decades characterize the majority of the membership. Regrettably, these changes suggest that successful intervention with such youth has become increasingly difficult to accomplish. Moore (1991) asserts that in the almost half-century since 1950, youth gang members in the United States have become (a) more entrenched in their communities, (b) more influential in the lives of their members, (c) more deviant in their behaviors, and (d) more socially isolated from other, nongang adolescent groups.

In companion with these changes is a discernable expansion of the age range in many youth gangs. In past decades, juvenile gangs consisted exclusively of youths, ages roughly 12 to 20. Today it is not uncommon for gang members to be in their 20s and even beyond. Klein (1995) describes this trend as the "graying of street gangs." Perhaps in part because less financial opportunity exists in this country's legitimate economy, and because more perceived if not real opportunity exists in its illegitimate economy, increasing numbers of youths are maintaining their gang affiliation beyond their teen years instead of jobbing-out, marrying-out, or aging-out. One serious implication of this phenomenon is the not inconsequential degree to which such veteran members may serve as undesirable role models for new or potential gang members.

Ethnicity and nationality of membership are further significant demographic features of the contemporary youth gang in the United States. Today, gangs include youths of African American, Hispanic, Asian, Caucasian, Russian, Albanian, El Salvadoran, Jamaican, Chinese, Vietnamese, Cambodian, Hmong, and other descent. Such diverse cultural roots have important consequences for our understanding of gang formation, behavior, and intervention in both school and community settings. Chapter 4 deals in depth with these themes.

INTERVENTIONS

Part 2 of this book describes state-of-the-art, best practices for gang intervention currently available in school and community settings. In the present chapter we provide a brief sketch of the history of gang intervention efforts to this point, as background for the more exhaustive presentation in Part 2.

Up to about the middle of this century, gang intervention was not of substantial concern in the United States. Youth gangs did exist, but they were viewed as "predatory play groups" whose spiritedness, roughhousing, or minor delinquencies (mostly vandalism and non-lethal fights) only occasionally got out of hand and required the attention of authorities. Gangs grew in number along with community concern in the period from 1950 to 1965. This was the era of the *detached worker approach* to gang intervention. Also termed *youth outreach* or *street gang work,* in this approach youth care agency personnel (mostly social workers) were urged to leave (detach from) their offices, stop requiring their clients to come to them, and get out into the neighborhoods and streets where gang youth congregated. There, on site, they would try to build relationships, assist in group problem solving, set standards for appropriate behavior, serve as prosocial models, encourage democratic decision making among the gang youth, and in other ways abet the overall goal of values transformation. It proved a popular approach, and detached worker programs appeared in a great many U.S. cities. However, as research became available evaluating the effectiveness of the detached worker approach (e.g., for reducing delinquent behavior), results were consistently unfavorable, and the approach largely faded from the gang scene of the day. Years later it became clear that in a great many cities the approach had, in fact, not been carried out in a real spirit of outreach. In Los Angeles, for example, "detached" workers still spent 50% of their time in their offices—25% traveling to the gang neighborhood and only 25% interacting with the youths (Klein, 1971). Given the size of caseloads, this translated to 5 minutes per youth per week! Thus, all that can be concluded at this point about the detached worker approach is that its effectiveness remains unknown.

In the following period, from approximately 1965 to 1975, the predominant approach to gang intervention in the U.S. was *opportunities provision.* Correctly, we believe, this approach incorporated the idea that certain attractions of gang membership (friendship, self-esteem, identity, excitement) reflect needs that can also be met by serious involvement in social, economic, recreational, and educational programming. This was the era of the War on Poverty. The names of a number of gang intervention programs embodying the spirit of opportunities provision concretize the thrust of the approach: Mobilization for Youth, Citywide Mural Project, Urban Leadership Training Program, Community Gang Service Project, Project New Pride, Youth Enterprise. Such a spirit is, unfortunately, no longer popular in this country. Part 2 of this book offers a description of exemplary contemporary school and community programs based on the idea of opportunities provision.

Beginning in the mid-1970s and continuing to the present time, a "get tough" approach to gang intervention predominated in the United States. In contrast to the opportunities provision/social infusion strategy, this new strategy was one of opportunities withdrawal/social control. No longer were social workers (for outreach work) or resource workers (for opportunities provision) the most common gang intervention personnel. Instead, the task fell to police, prosecutors, judges, and other criminal justice workers. And why not? Gang behavior was no longer the vandalism and minor delinquencies of the past. Gang youth (like much of the rest of the country) were arming themselves, and doing so with ever-more-lethal weapons. Some (though not many) were involved in street-level drug trafficking and used their weapons to solidify their drug enterprise rights. More frequently, gang territoriality was being expressed by drive-by shootings or other lethal mayhem. The public became increasingly frightened and outraged, demanded a harsh response, and got it. Today in the United States the bulk of gang work consists of surveillance, investigation, deterrence, suppression, arrest, prosecution, and incarceration.

We believe strongly that this approach toward gang intervention is grossly inadequate and ultimately self-defeating. In no field of human intervention work does "one size fit all." What we have elsewhere called "one-true-light prescriptions" (Goldstein & Stein, 1976) serve the intervenor's needs more than the youth's needs. Earlier, we noted that many different types of youth groups are labeled as gangs in the United States today, and an equally diverse array of youths are viewed and dealt with as gang members. Correspondingly, we must seek an equally broad array of effective interventions. The suppression strategy must be replaced by a comprehensive strategy, one that includes but goes well beyond the suppression methods currently in favor. In school settings, interventions must at minimum be of three types: in-school safety and control procedures, in-school enrichment procedures, and formal linkages to community-based interventions. School gang intervention programs incorporating all three of these classes of intervention have the potential to suppress inappropriate behaviors and to enhance desirable behaviors in both school and community settings. The chapters in Part 2 of this book provide a full description of programs concretizing this comprehensive gang intervention strategy.

SUMMARY

This introduction has illustrated the complexity involved in the seemingly simple task of reaching a shared definition of *gang*. Such complexity grows from the realization that the label fits many differing types of youth groups—some in existence very briefly, others enduring for decades. Gang membership is similarly complex, with some youths joining early in their lives and remaining well beyond adolescence, and others merely "visiting" for one or more short periods. We have also sketched a general view of gangs and gang member demographics, as well as summarized the history of gang intervention efforts over the past 50 years. This overview of gang, member, and intervention characteristics is a prelude to more detailed consideration in the following chapters.

Part 1
Gangs Come to School

CHAPTER ONE

District, School, & Classroom Characteristics

Any of the 16,000 school districts, 84,000 schools, and several hundred thousand classrooms in the United States can become the incubation site for a youth gang. The time is long past when students and others viewed school as neutral turf, exempt from crime, violence, and gang-banging. Educators are both dismayed and surprised at this serious change in the character of U.S. schools. We share the dismay, but not the surprise. If anything, we are surprised that for so many decades schools *were* neutral turf. After all, schools in other ways reflect the communities of which they are a part. As the numbers of gangs and the level of gang violence grew on our streets, in our parks, and in our back alleys, it was inevitable that the same would happen in the place our youth gather most frequently: our schools.

While gangs can and have formed anywhere (urban, suburban, rural), at all socioeconomic levels, in all ethnicities, and in all geographic locations, gangs are not equally likely to develop in each of these venues. In the present chapter, we describe and examine characteristics of school districts, schools, and classrooms that appear to be associated with both high and low levels of gang activity.

THE DISTRICT

While the presence of groups of adolescents or preadolescents causing mayhem in the United States is as old as the country itself, serious concern about the behavior of such youngsters first emerged in the mid-1800s, as children of newly arrived Italian, Irish, or Jewish immigrants banded together within each of their respective neighborhoods for play and for protection of their turf from one another's real and imagined incursions. These were all children of poor parents, parents struggling long hours to adjust to a new and strange land. The parents often were unavailable to their children or, even if available, frequently less knowledgeable about the new culture and its demands than the youngsters themselves, for whom compulsory school attendance brought daily exposure to the realities of language and living in this country.

These neighborhoods—first in New York City, the "gateway to America," and later in Chicago, Boston, Philadelphia, and elsewhere—shared the characteristics of poor neighborhoods everywhere, then and now. Recreational opportunities provided by the community were minimal or nonexistent. There were no or very few parks, community centers, or playgrounds. Fun to be had was fun to be made. Competition for access to limited resources became a major force in generating and defining the groups of youth who became gangs. Perhaps it should not surprise us that one early researcher described such gangs as "predatory play groups" (Thrasher, 1927/1963). Jobs were hard to come by for these youths' parents, and even less available for the youngsters themselves. Housing was inadequate—crowded, dingy, of poor construction, sometimes dangerous. Sanitation, medical care, and nutrition were often markedly substandard.

Life was clearly hard for the immigrant youngsters of this era and their families. And it was not only the difficulties of their physical environment that made it so. The Statue of Liberty may have bade them welcome, but far too often their already established neighbors did not. Cultural barriers and prejudices, clenched hands saying "go away" rather than open arms of welcome, characterized much of their daily experience. As so often happens when there is an out-group, threatening "them," for these youths there was a coalescing, in-group "us": the gang protecting them.

One hundred and fifty years later, the scenario remains much the same. Skin color may have changed some, but not much else. Limited access to opportunities for work or play, the dismal conditions of daily living, poor adult supervision, the threat and hostility of rival gangs, and the barriers regularly imposed by the prevailing culture still characterize the world from which most youth gangs emerge. Today they and their neighborhoods are no longer largely Italian, Irish, or Jewish. Youth gangs in the U.S. in the late 1900s are mostly African American or Hispanic/Latino. The minority of gangs that are otherwise composed are almost entirely of youth from one or another newly arrived immigrant group: Russian, Jamaican, El Salvadoran, Somali, Vietnamese, Albanian, Chinese. Who will be our gang youth a hundred years from now? Almost certainly, they primarily will be poor youngsters, youngsters from families having difficulty being admitted to the legitimate economy, youngsters living in poor housing and receiving inadequate medical care, nutrition, recreational opportunities, and the like.

Neighborhoods fertile for the development of youth gangs, and for more general criminal behavior, have been shown to possess a number of features in addition to the economic and social deprivation just described. They may be socially disorganized areas, showing considerable instability, population turnover, mobility, and outmigration of the middle classes. Some may evidence stability, but this stability is fragile and rests upon a subculture of agreed-upon conventional as well as antisocial norms, beliefs, and behaviors. Miller (1958), for example, early on described lower socioeconomic communities whose cultural traditions were toughness, trouble, smartness, excitement, fate, and autonomy. These neighborhoods often also contained only a few persons and institutions that might serve as controls on inappropriate behaviors or as resources reflecting alternative, positive routes to life goals. The high percentage of female-headed households, the relative scarcity of positive role models and mentors, and poor supervision of youth exemplify this characteristically negative neighborhood.

While the bulk of youth gang members in the U.S. are as we have previously described, a small but significant number are neither ethnic or national minorities, nor of lower socioeconomic status. If most youth gangs stem from the conditions of poverty and discrimination, why do suburban, middle-class school districts also increasingly report the presence and growth of youth gangs? These more affluent youth share the personal motivations that propel low-income youths toward gang involvement. These qualities, examined at length in chapter 3, include a need for peer friendship, pride, identity development, self-esteem, resource acquisition, and excitement. Sadly, these youngsters often share harsh discipline, poor supervision, and little parental involvement. They also share more, especially a culture driven by the mass media.

Language, food preferences, clothing styles, grooming styles, activity preferences, music (both enjoyed and disparaged), dances, and more constitute the ever-changing youth culture in this country. This culture spreads as rapidly as film, television, and other mass media channels can portray it. Among the many fashions thus widely and quickly disseminated are gang clothing ("gangster chic"), gang affectations (slang, strut walking), and gang creation itself. It is clear, then, that youth gangs in the United States may form in any school district, regardless of the predominant social class, national origin, or ethnicity of its student body. Some districts are more at risk than others, but none can assume "it can't happen here."

THE SCHOOL

Let us begin this section in positive terms by describing the several features of contemporary U.S. schools associated with low levels of gang development and operation. The opposite features, the reader may infer, promote or covary with the growth and presence of youth gangs.

As noted, youths join gangs for many reasons, one of which may be described fairly as the common adolescent goal of community seeking. Members frequently describe their gang as "family" and express loyalty by saying they are "being down for the homeboys." Such statements of intense commitment, cohesiveness, and attraction to group exemplify adolescent striving for community. To the degree that the school or conventional adolescent peer group are experienced by youths as a valuable community, there may be, for some youths, that much less pull toward the gang. Does the school and its various substructures or subcultures have a deep and broad sense of a collective "us," rather than disassociation, marginalization, or a sense of "them" (staff) versus "us" (students)? A sense of community in schools grows from several factors, particularly school size, governance, curriculum, and safety.

Size

Five out of every six secondary schools in the United States have 2,500 or more students (Goldstein & Conoley, 1997). Fewer than one out of six contain the recommended number of 600 to 800 students. At levels in this latter range, it is possible for principals and vice principals to be visible to all students, to know students by name, and by other means to personalize staff-student relationships in ways that enhance the students' sense of belonging, even if only by being greeted and called by name at the schoolhouse door. Size, however, relates to community building in an even more significant manner. Too large a student body increases the chances of impersonality or even anonymity and of crowding-associated arguments or fights. It also makes it more likely that poorly performing students, who may already be more attracted to gang membership, may become even more marginalized by being disconnected from the school. All schools, regardless of size, have at most one band, one football team, one chorus. That is, the number of roles for students that might help them feel part of the larger school community is finite and often insufficient to engage marginalized youth. In small schools, one or more roles are likely to exist for all who wish to participate. In large schools, some students will find none. Alienation, not community, is the result.

Governance

How is the school run? Ample research supports the value of "fair but firm" participatory leadership, in contrast to leadership that is either too autocratic or too permissive. Schools fostering a sense of community regularly use shared decision making. Principals and vice principals do not abdicate their leadership roles—the buck still stops at their desks. But final decisions on an array of school matters are not made until full and open consultation with the parties affected by the decision is complete. Teachers, students, parents, and others are actively sought out; their thinking is engaged and seriously factored into any final decisions. What a tremendous boost to a shared sense of community! Too often, unfortunately, in schools today "shared decision making" is characterized by an administration's autonomously making relevant decisions, then sharing them with staff and students. Little in the sense of "we-ness" follows from such autocracy.

A sense of school as community is also advanced by the administration's fair and consistent response to grievances, whether made by teachers, students, parents, or others. Protests about decisions or actions are responded to openly and considered on their merits. Open channels of communication about these and other important school matters also characterize low-risk schools. Not only does information flow freely and regularly down the chain—administration to teacher to student—it also travels in the reverse direction. Good administrators know what is happening (or is about to happen) in their own schools.

With particular relevance to gang development, community-enhancing administrators are secure enough about their own competence to avoid denying to themselves as well as to others that one or more gangs exist in their schools. Too often the confirming evidence of graffiti, hand signs, clothing, or colors is minimized, misinterpreted, or denied from fear that the school board, taxpayers, parents, or others will view the gang presence as a reflection of administrative incompetence. Quite the contrary, we believe: The first step in any successful gang intervention effort is acknowledgment that gangs have indeed come to the school. We live in a global village in which almost instantaneous communication facilitates the rapid spread of all aspects of youth culture: dress, language, leisure preferences, and, indeed, gang involvement. Denial and inertia in the early phases of gang development are the first steps on a slippery slope toward permanent gang presence in the school and community.

Curriculum

A school's sense of community also may be enhanced substantially by certain qualities of its curriculum. Later chapters on gang intervention programming will focus on curricular enrichment and its relevance to the real-world needs of both gang and nongang youth. Here, we wish to mention that aspect of school curriculum most relevant to a sense of belonging.

Many schools today look more and more like miniature United Nations. Different ethnicities, languages, cultures, and learning styles increasingly characterize our students. To reach such a diverse student body and to pull its disparate cultural parts into a meaningful whole, skilled administrators and teachers develop and deliver a curriculum that is both appropriate and appreciative. Curricular substance and manner of presentation are consistent with and responsive to the diverse backgrounds and learning styles represented (i.e., "appropriate"), as well as developed and revised in active and continuing consultation with persons representing the cultural groups to be taught (i.e., "appreciative").

Safety

Finally, and perhaps most basically, in addition to its size, governance, and curriculum, a school's sense of community grows from its safety. Fear, intimidation, bullying, harassment, and danger are the antithesis of community. Such a conclusion is perhaps obvious. Less obvious, however, is the likelihood that many of the steps taken by school administrators to enhance school safety also decrease student and staff sense of community. We refer in particular to the heavy reliance in U.S. schools on technology to ensure security. Consider the perspective of a typical middle-school student for a moment:

> You arrive at school after a half-hour school bus trip during which a red light on a video camera bolted over the bus's front window has informed you that your every move has been recorded. Getting off the bus, you spot one of your school's three full-time police officers posted by the front entrance. You stand on line a few minutes, waiting to pass through the school's metal detector. As you wait, another student several places ahead of you passes through and is pulled out, some sort of weapon discovered inside his jacket. Glancing back toward the buses, you see the physical education teacher at the curb in the middle of the crowd of just-arrived students. You wonder why

he's holding a TV minicam. You pass through the metal detector—carrying the mesh, see-through bookbag containing your books—and walk down the corridor on your way to your home room. The lockers that used to be there before have all been removed.

While such unwelcoming scenes are not yet the rule, they are becoming increasingly common. Does this entrance to a typical school day in many schools in the U.S. feel like a "welcome to your community"? We think not, and we urge that the gang management cure not prove worse than the disease! While highly visible physical security is often necessary and prudent, school safety can be enhanced in ways that foster, rather than diminish, a sense of community. Among these approaches are a school mission statement developed not by administration alone, but in full collaboration with staff, parents, and students; codes of rights and responsibilities, also jointly developed; dress codes, including use of school uniforms; the rapid removal of graffiti and repair of vandalism; substantial, schoolwide programming to prevent bullying and harassment; and the incorporation into regular curricular offerings of gang prevention and gang awareness information. Technology and security personnel certainly have a place in a comprehensive school safety program, but their contribution must be balanced by measures designed to facilitate, not impede, the all-important sense of community at the heart of gang management programming.

THE CLASSROOM

Community Building

Community building optimally continues, and even expands, as we move from the building to the classroom level. It is common in schools with no gang presence for teachers to spend a considerable amount of time at the beginning of the school term creating a sense of "we-ness." Teacher effort is devoted to instilling a climate of cooperation and collaboration among students, rather than indifference to or competition with one another. Curriculum is not ignored during these early efforts to enhance group identity; however, curriculum may be of secondary importance, looked on as more of a vehicle for the goal of community building than as an academic target in its own right. All students in the room learn one another's names; share information in order to discuss likes, strengths, and similarities; participate in activities involving the whole class; and, on occasion, engage in games and simulations to enhance cooperation.

Curricular Content

For too many youngsters, school days are "school daze." Much of what is being taught seems quite aside from their daily lives and their future aspirations. When asked, they complain that school is boring, boring, boring. The impact of perceived irrelevance on aggression has been suggested by a number of researchers. Csikszentmihalyi and Larsen (1978), for example, in proposing their enjoyment theory of vandalism, note that a large percentage of students find their school experiences to be especially boring and irrelevant to their planned life goals. These students often respond to such boredom and irrelevance with acts of vandalism directed toward the institution they perceive as the source. In this context, it is relevant to note that greatly expanded vocational education opportunities might diminish this sense of irrelevance and boredom; however, as a nation we have collectively offered these opportunities to fewer and fewer students.

Managing the Classroom

Kounin's (1970) observations, as well as our own (Goldstein, Palumbo, Striepling, & Voutsinas, 1995) suggest a set of particularly important teacher behaviors, all relevant to creating a gang-free environment.

First, the teacher knows what is going on. Such *with-it-ness* is communicated to the class in a number of ways, including swift and consistent recognition and, when necessary, consequating of low-level behaviors likely to grow into disruptiveness or more serious aggression. Closely connected to such attentiveness is *overlapping,* the ability to simultaneously manage two or more classroom events, be they instructional or disciplinary. *Smoothness,* the ability to transition from one activity to another without "down time," is a third facilitative teacher behavior. Down time is a good time for boredom-engendered acting out; avoiding or minimizing it significantly deters such behaviors. Another way to minimize boredom is by instructing with *momentum,* or maintaining a steady sense of progress or movement throughout a particular lesson, class, or school day. A *group focus,* the ability to keep the entire class involved in a given instructional activity, also characterizes a classroom free of conflict. Finally, and especially significant, is the communication by the teacher of consistently *optimistic expectations.* Students live up to (and, unfortunately, also down to) what important people in their lives expect of them. The teacher who expects an eighth grader to read at fifth-grade level because of his or her past record, or a sibling's past poor performance in the same school, or the neighborhood the student comes from will likely be rewarded with fifth-grade performance. By contrast, the teacher who, in the wide variety of ways available to teachers, lets the student know he or she can achieve and will have the teacher's energetic help to do so along the way is likely to motivate the student to be more academically successful, more involved, and, one would hope, less attracted to gangs.

Rules and Procedures

Teachers with few gang problems in their classrooms teach rules and procedures as explicitly as they teach academic content. Rules are guidelines governing appropriate and inappropriate student behaviors. Procedures are what students need to know and follow in order to meet their own personal needs and to perform routine instructional and classroom housekeeping activities. Effective teachers integrate their rules and procedures—as well as consequences for failing to follow them—into their classroom routines. A good set of "rules for rules" are that they be (a) few in number, (b) negotiated with the students, (b) stated behaviorally, (c) stated positively, (d) sent home to parents, and (e) posted in the classroom. As with rules, classroom procedures need to be explicitly taught; one cannot assume that students know them. Unlike rules, which should be taught "up front," procedures for obtaining help, leaving the room, using bathroom passes, disposing of trash, and so forth usually can be explained as the need arises. As with rules, however, procedures need to be clearly stated, closely monitored, consistently followed, and consequated when not followed.

Home-School Collaboration

Schools have always sought home-school contact, but many times contact has meant the schools' (the experts) telling the parents (the nonexperts) what to do. Traditionally, contact has taken the form of PTA meetings, parent-teacher conferences, or, as far too often has been the case with youngsters prone to gang affiliation, the "bad news" call, in which someone from the school phones home to tell the parents, in effect, what a lousy kid they have. Teachers in classrooms with no gang presence often view and deal with parents quite differently. They recognize and appreciate parents as the youth's first (and ongoing) teacher, and they seek contact early and frequently, seeing this contact as an opportunity to collaborate in a supportive, mutually reinforcing way. Enacting such an attitude helps create the opportunity for the parents, the teacher, and, it is hoped, the student to become a sort of problem-solving team. The opportunity for the student to be successful in school is enhanced, and gang participation becomes correspondingly less attractive.

Learning from Teachers
in High-Aggression Schools

Finally, teachers may make a major contribution toward keeping their classrooms gang-free if they vigorously avoid several behaviors suggested by Remboldt (1994) that serve as enablers, not inhibitors, of student aggression:

△ Ignoring student complaints of being threatened

△ Avoiding high-violence school locations

△ Ignoring low-level violence (put-downs, bullying, harassment)

△ Ignoring student threats of planned violence

△ Ignoring rumors about students who may have weapons

△ Failing to intervene or report witnessed student violence

△ Excusing violent behavior of "good kids" as necessary for self-defense

GANGS IN YOUR SCHOOL

Thus far in this chapter we have described qualities of school districts, schools, and classrooms relevant to the likelihood that youth gangs will develop and grow. Our emphasis has been on the positive—in particular, the school and classroom characteristics making gang creation and public presence substantially less likely. What about *your* school? How likely is it that a gang presence has already been, or is likely to be, established in *your* district, school, or classroom? The remaining chapters in Part 1 of this book provide information to help answer this crucial question accurately; we progressively describe gang signs and symbols, recruitment, ethnicity, and violence in U.S. schools today. After reading chapters 2 through 5, you will be able to estimate quite adequately your own gang circumstances and thus the degree to which your site ought to actively pursue one or more of the effective interventions described in Part 2, chapters 6 through 8.

As a first step in this assessment process, we provide in Table 3 the Gang Assessment Tool, developed by the National School Safety Center (Stephens, 1992). Consider it an informal measure of your site's gang involvement, a measure still being developed psychometrically. Anecdotally, it provides a reasonable starting point for estimating your own situation. Accompanying the measure are suggested levels of response as a function of the total score.

SUMMARY

Youth gang development is advanced or retarded by a host of contextual characteristics. Some are qualities of the community in which potential and actual gang members reside. Others are features of the schools and classrooms those youths attend. We have described these membership-promoting and membership-inhibiting characteristics in order to give a fuller sense of the environments in which gang attraction or avoidance may emerge. We also suggest that actively enhancing aspects of the latter environments is likely to reduce the numbers of youth to whom gang membership is appealing.

Table 3—Gang Assessment Tool

1. Do you have graffiti on or near your campus? 5 points

2. Do you have crossed-out graffiti on or near your campus? 5 points

3. Do your students wear colors, jewelry, clothing, flash hand signs, or display other behavior that may be gang related? 10 points

4. Are drugs available at or near your school? 5 points

5. Has a significant increase occurred in the number of physical confrontations/ stare-downs within the past 12 months in or near your school? 5 points

6. Are weapons increasingly present in your community? 10 points

7. Are beepers, pagers, or cellular phones used by your students? 10 points

8. Have you had a drive-by shooting at or around your school? 15 points

9. Have you had a "show-by" display of weapons at or around your school? 10 points

10. Is your truancy rate increasing? 5 points

11. Are an increasing number of racial incidents occurring in your community or school? 5 points

12. Does your community have a history of gangs? 10 points ✔

13. Is there an increasing presence of "informal social groups" with unusual (aggressive, territorial) names? 15 points

Note. From "Gangs vs. Schools: Assessing the Score in Your Community" by Ronald D. Stephens, March 1992, *School Safety Update* (National School Safety Center News Service), p. 8. Adapted by permission.

Table 3—Gang Assessment Tool CONTINUED

Total Score

15 or less:	No significant gang problem exists.
20 to 40:	An emerging gang problem; monitoring and development of a gang plan is recommended.
45 to 60:	Gang problem exists. Establish and implement a systematic gang prevention and intervention plan.
65 or more:	Acute gang problem exists, meriting a total prevention, intervention, and suppression effort.

CHAPTER TWO

Signs & Symbols

Most adolescents in this country will, with considerable energy and emotional investment, seek to belong to a group of like-minded, value-sharing peers. For many it will be an informal group, with minimal structure, providing many hours of time together. For others it may be an athletic club, a social club, or a formal group from school, a religious institution, or a community center. Some will join a gang.

These seemingly diverse groups, at their core, all provide their members with the opportunity to accomplish two exceedingly desirable goals. The first is to be a member of a cohesive group, sharing time, space, interests, activities, purpose, and often appearance. Group membership provides the opportunity to declare to all who will listen: "I am a member" and "We are an 'us'." The companion goal is distinctiveness—from all other clubs, teams, informal groups, or gangs. Here declared is difference from all others: "They are a 'them'." These complementary goals of sameness and difference, in-group and out-group, are intensely experienced by most adolescents, and none more so than by the members of the contemporary youth gang, whom we have elsewhere described as "hyperadolescents" (Goldstein, 1991). Klein (1995) has taken a similar view in his description of such youngsters as "a caricature of adolescence" and "adolescence overplayed."

By what routes may these dual goals be reached? For gang members, the means are many, varied, and ever changing. Membership, and hence both in-group sameness and out-group difference, may be signified especially by graffiti, hand signs, tattoos, and clothing (the items themselves, their brand, and how they are worn). In some instances gang affiliation is indicated by jewelry, hairstyles, and decoration of fingernails; use of certain words, phrases, and speaking styles; the assumption of particular postures; and the conspicuous flashing of money, goods, drugs, or weapons. The nature and often multiple purposes of these gang signs and symbols are described in the present chapter.

GRAFFITI

Gang graffiti vandalism is the painting, spraying, or carving of gang or gang member initials, names, symbols, or street locations on walls, signs, trucks, and a wide variety of other locations. Also taking the form of self-laudatory and rival-deprecating comments, this type of vandalism is committed most frequently to affirm identity (i.e., sameness and difference from all others) and may in fact serve other purposes as well, as listed in Table 4. Figure 2 illustrates a number of these purposes.

Table 4—Purposes of Gang Graffiti

1. Affirm gang identity
2. Affirm member identity
3. Mark territorial ownership rights
4. Issue a challenge (give notice)
5. Memorialize deceased members (own gang)
6. Disrespect deceased members (other gang)
7. Celebrate violent incidents
8. List intended victims
9. Intimidate rival gang or community

Figure 2—Multipurpose Gang Graffiti

OG/SNIPER

8/3

HC

SUR

B/K

The gang member responsible for the graffiti in Figure 2, whose name or moniker is Sniper, claims to be an "OG" or an old or original gangster (i.e., a founding member of the gang or at least a long-time member). The location of the gang is 83rd Street ("8/3"), and its name is the Hoover Crips ("HC"), a Crip gang located in the Hoover section of Los Angeles. The "SUR" represents Southern California, and "B/K" gives notice that the writer is a Blood Killer and challenges and "disses" any Blood gang members who happen by.

Some gang graffiti are simply crude paintings of the gang's initials (Figure 3) or name (Figure 4); others are an elaborate portrayal of the gang's symbol (Figure 5). They typically appear on street-level walls but gain status among their perpetrators the more inaccessible the site on which they are placed.

Today as in past years, youth gangs in this country are centrally preoccupied with establishing, maintaining, and at times expanding their territory, turf, or "hood." Graffiti are often employed by gang members as public notification of such territoriality. Functionally, such "planting the flag" resembles the widespread practice of publicly posting one's privately owned land as a means of saying, "I own this—stay off" (see Figure 6).

Figure 3—Gang Initials: West Side S.G. Crips

Figure 4—Gang Name: 30's Blood Gang

Figure 5—Gang Symbol: Latin Kings

Figure 6—Posted: No Trespassing

The memorializing, commemorative function of gang graffiti is evident as praise for deceased members of one's own gang (i.e., a "Wall of Heaven" or an "R.I.P. [Rest in Peace] Wall"; Figure 7) or as disrespect (by crossing out or drawing upside down) for living or deceased members of a rival gang (i.e., a "Wall of Hell"; Figure 8). In a similar manner, an entire rival gang can be "dissed" by graffiti of its name crossed out or upside down (Figure 9), or its symbol similarly treated (Figure 10).

In school settings, graffiti of these several types may appear on exterior, corridor, classroom, office, or bathroom walls; desks; clothing; textbooks and notebooks; chalkboards; bulletin boards; cafeteria tables; the insides of lockers; chairs; and any and all other accessible surfaces.

Figure 7—Wall of Heaven: Tears of a Clown

**Figure 8—Wall of Hell: Bogus Boy Killer
and Mickey Cobra Killer**

Figure 9—Graffiti Wall with Numerous Cross-outs

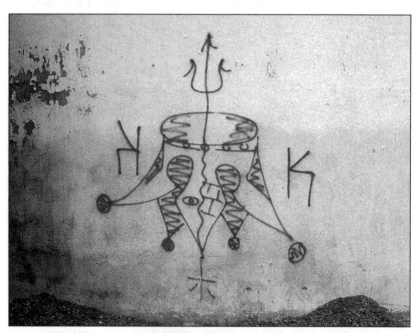

**Figure 10—Upside Down Gang Symbol:
Latin Kings**

HAND SIGNS

As is true for graffiti, gang hand signs usually depict the gang's name, initials, or symbol. Hand signs are employed for several purposes (Table 5), though as for graffiti, their function is primarily to affirm "I am a member." Figures 11 through 13, respectively, signify membership in the Bishops, Gangster Disciples, and West Side Gang. Figures 14 and 15, respectively, portray the hand signs of a Crip gang and a Blood gang.

One's own gang's hand sign, therefore, may be used to communicate membership or to challenge perceived gang rivals. Some gangs are quite large, and membership turnover can be substantial. Thus, knowing who is or is not a member of a rival gang may at times be a puzzle, perhaps a dangerous puzzle. "False flagging" (i.e., throwing a rival gang's hand sign correctly), if responded to in kind, confirms to the flagger that the other is indeed from a rival gang. Alternatively, one may know the other is from a rival gang and wish to show disrespect or issue a challenge. In a manner parallel to redrawing a rival gang's graffiti upside down, such contempt or challenge may be conveyed by throwing the rival's sign upside down.

Table 5—Purposes of Gang Hand Signs

1. Communicate gang affiliation (throwing own sign)
2. Challenge rival gang members (throwing own sign)
3. Identify rival gang members (throwing rival sign correctly— "false flagging")
4. Show contempt for or challenge rival gang members (throwing rival sign upside down)

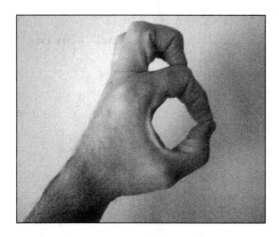

Figure 11—
**Bishops Hand
Sign**

Figure 12—
**Gangster
Disciples Hand
Sign**

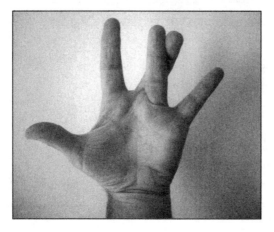

Figure 13—
**West Side Gang
Hand Sign**

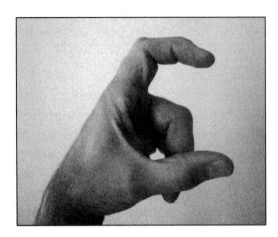

**Figure 14—
Hand Sign of
Crip Gang**

**Figure 15—
Hand Sign of
Blood Gang**

TATTOOS

In-group affiliation and out-group differences may also be signified by the presence and absence of body tattoos. As we have seen with other signs and symbols, tattoos may serve several purposes, listed in Table 6 in likely order of frequency. Gang members' tattoos typically appear on the arms or chest; sometimes on the neck, hands, fingers, or ankles. A teardrop tattoo below the eye often commemorates a deceased fellow gang member. Figures 16 through 18 illustrate, respectively, gang member tattoos from the Oriental Ruthless Boys, the Crips, and the Gangster Disciples.

Table 6—Purposes of Gang Tattoos

1. Affirm gang identity
2. Memorialize a deceased member
3. Commemorate a special gang event
4. Commemorate date gang was formed (especially in motorcycle gangs)

Figure 16—Oriental Ruthless Boys Tattoo

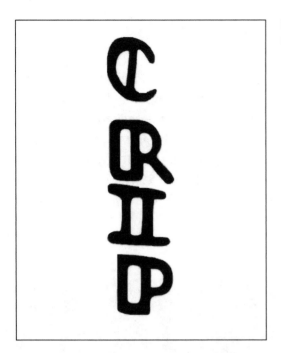

Figure 17—
Crips Tattoo

Figure 18—
Gangster
Disciples Tattoo

CLOTHING

Many adolescents proclaim their group alliance (with peers) and individuality (from others) with what they wear and how they wear it. Adolescents belonging to gangs, earlier described as hyperadolescents, do so also, and then some. In many ways, clothes *are* their statement. All items of clothing can be used for gang-signifying purposes, including especially caps (Figure 19), jackets (Figure 20), T-shirts (Figure 21), and jewelry (Figure 22).

Figure 19—Lao Boyz Cap

**Figure 20—
Los Angeles
Gang Jackets**

**Figure 21—
Gangster
Disciples Nation
T-Shirt**

**Figure 22—
Girls' Vice Lord
Toy Jewelry**

SCHOOL RESPONSES

Schools in many locations throughout the United States have responded to graffiti, hand signs, tattoos, and gang-signifying clothing with persuasion, prohibition with punishment for violations, and the provision of alternatives.

Persuasive attempts have included codes of conduct, well-disseminated to students and parents; ongoing schoolwide or districtwide anti-gang campaigns, including assemblies, announcements, and posters, letters home to parents (Figures 24 and 25) and other components; student orientation handbooks; and school safety plans.

Prohibition with punishment for violation has included dress codes, illustrated by the composite shown in Table 7; school rule

Figure 23—Sample Letter to Inform Parents/Guardians of Possible Gang-Related Activity

Date _____

Dear parents or guardians of _____ :

As you are probably aware, gang violence is a problem in our city. Threats, intimidation, fights, beatings, and shootings are common when rival gang members meet. Unfortunately, many school-age youths find gangs fascinating. Some students regularly interact with older gang members. Some students are themselves involved in gangs. For others, it is popular to dress, talk, and act like active gang members, even when they are not. This can cause serious or even life-threatening problems when such "imitators" or marginal gang members encounter real, some- times armed, gang members. Violent interactions have occurred around and in our school as a result of the display of gang colors, use of hand signs, and exchange of gang slang among students and others. To enhance student safety, we have a zero-tolerance policy regarding gang dress, talk, graffiti, and hand-signing in our school.

This letter is being written to inform you that your child has been engaging in some behavior in school that may be gang related. We have counseled your child to stop all such activity immediately. Further activity may lead to suspension from school if it poses a provable, immediate gang threat or relates to gang intimidation. Criminal gang activity will be referred to the police.

Please speak with your child about the dangers of real or pretend gang involvement. Any of your child's teachers, the school social worker, or I would welcome a phone call from you. Please contact one of us as soon as possible.

Sincerely,

Principal

Figure 24—Sample Letter to Inform Parents/Guardians of Graffiti Vandalism

Date _____

Dear parents or guardians of _____ :

Providing a safe and respectable environment is our first and most important task when educating young people. Positive discipline and strong academic expectations can be achieved only when the physical environment is safe, clean, and presentable. We are requesting your active assistance in maintaining such an environment at our school.

Recently, we have begun experiencing significant problems with students' writing graffiti in the building. Often the graffiti consist of students' writing their names on walls, on posters, in the toilets, and on desks and textbooks. Increasingly, the graffiti also depict gang logos, threats, and slogans. We remove all graffiti we see within minutes of discovery, but we need your help in reducing graffiti even further.

Your son or daughter does not need any indelible markers at school. Please do not allow your child to bring such markers to school unless your child's classroom teacher specifically asks you by letter to send them. If your son or daughter has folders, note-books, or books marked with writing that you do not understand, please ask your child the meaning of such writing. Call us if you have any specific concerns regarding graffiti.

Also, please be aware that any graffiti that result in expense to the district through damage to school property may be recorded as vandalism and reported to the police department.

Thank you for your support. Please feel free to call if you have any suggestions, questions, or recommendations for making our school a safer place.

Sincerely,

Principal

setting and disciplinary penalties, such as lost privileges and suspension; monetary fines; restitution; and student vandalism accounts.

Provision of alternatives has been concretized by schoolwide and
districtwide requirements for school uniforms; the use of school-
approved murals and other graffiti dissuaders; and voluntary (and
free) tattoo-removal programs.

Table 7—Common School Dress Code Targets

Gold jewelry

Multi-fingered rings

Gold dental caps

Baggy pants

Ripped jeans

Elastic ankle gathers

Underwear worn as outerwear

Skirts or shorts above knees

Tank tops

Muscle shirts

Halters

See-through blouses

Sex/drug message T-shirts

Doc Martens combat-style boots

Selected team jackets

Hats/caps

Sneakers with heel lights

SUMMARY

The powerful need to differentiate "us" from "them" is characteristic of all adolescents. Such striving for in-group solidarity, combined with an acute response to differences from all out-groups, perhaps reaches its zenith in juvenile gangs. In so much of their attitudes and behaviors, they are "hyperadolescents." A variety of words, signs, and symbols become the vehicles to declare sameness and demean rival gang differences, as well as to define and reinforce gang affinity. These manifestations include graffiti, hand signs, tattoos, clothing, jewelry, and more. In the present chapter we have described a sample of such signifiers, noted their diverse purposes, and illustrated the types of preventive and deterrent responses used by schools in the United States today.

CHAPTER THREE

Becoming a Gang Member

MEMBERSHIP MOTIVATIONS

In years past, a youth may have joined an athletic club, the school choir, a social club, or another formal or informal adolescent group because there was a good match between what the youth was seeking and what the group offered. Joining brings a sense of *belonging* and the chance to be part of the in-group. Belonging enhances *pride, self-esteem,* and the development of one's own *identity,* three additional adolescent goals deriving from in-group membership. Belonging provides opportunities for recreation, friendship, and sometimes economic gain.

As is true for the athletic club, the choir, the social club, and all other adolescent groupings, the youth gang offers the chance to belong. In the case of many gangs, joining may provide added benefits for the new member in terms of opportunities for both *excitement* and the acquisition of *resources* (i.e., objects, money, relationships) otherwise less available. Under school or neighborhood circumstances in which there is considerable pressure on the youth to join, doing so serves to *eliminate peer pressure* and enhance a perception, albeit false, of increased security.

Belonging, pride, self-esteem, identity enhancement, excitement, resources, and removal of peer pressure are in fact the membership motivations regularly identified by gang researchers. It is important to stress that these reasons for joining a gang are healthy, typical adolescent motivations, yet to emphasize that being in the gang is ultimately counterproductive and dangerous. As our later discussion of intervention programming in Part 2 will emphasize, the pull of gang membership is reduced to the degree that these same youth goals can be met by positive social, educational, recreational, or vocational offerings in the school or community and to the extent that the youth perceives these to be acceptable.

Other motivations for seeking gang membership have been cited. Spergel (1995) suggests the need for recognition, status, safety, power, money, and new experiences. Jankowski (1991) adds the desire for material incentives, recreation, refuge and camouflage, and physical protection, as well as the preprogrammed nature of all adolescents to rebel, resist, and seek paths different from those urged upon them by the adults in their lives. Indeed, youths join gangs for motivations that are numerous, varied, and complex.

If these motivations are held both by youngsters who join gangs and by those who seek their fulfillment via nongang peer groups, what determines which path will be followed? Curry and Spergel (1992) propose that risk factors predisposing the choice to affiliate with a gang are known association with gang members; presence of gangs in one's neighborhood or school; having a relative who is a gang member; a history of drug abuse; and a delinquency record, particularly for aggressive acts.

Padilla (1992) stresses that those electing gang membership often never have the chance to vote. Taking a view derived from labeling theory, he proposes that

> Their affirmative judgment of the gang and decision to
> join were developed over time as contact and interaction
> with teachers and some school mates already familiar
> with or actually belonging to gangs resulted in their being
> labeled "deviants" and troublemakers and treated accord-
> ingly. (p. 72)

Finally, Klein (1995) suggests that the characteristics of those who join gangs, as opposed to those who do not, include the following:

◁ A group of substantial personal deficiencies, such as low self-esteem, poor school performance, inadequate impulse control, and deficient social skills

◁ A marked tendency to employ defiance and violence, accompanied by pride in physical prowess

◁ An above-average desire for power, status, and companionship

◁ A boring, unexciting, often isolated life-style

The membership motivations just cited represent the views of experts-by-credentials (i.e., gang researchers) regarding the personal and environmental reasons youths join gangs. What do experts-by-experience (i.e., ex-gang members themselves) say are the reasons for affiliation? According to an extensive survey of such respondents conducted by Spergel (1995), the reasons youths give for joining gangs concern availability, fun, friendship, protection, lack of home supervision, having an older brother in a gang, ignorance of the downside of membership, status, and power. Clearly, the attractions associated with joining a youth gang are, for many youngsters, diverse, powerful, and often compelling.

RECRUITMENT

With all that gang membership has going for it in the eyes of the prospect, how does the recruitment process actually unfold? Jankowski (1991) describes three alternatives. *Fraternity* appears most common, and is thus named for its general similarity to the fraternity or sorority rush: "Let's hang out together—if we like you and you like us, you're invited in." Youths growing up in a neighborhood and going to the same neighborhood schools have ample opportunities for such reciprocal exposure and thus, in a sense, simply grow into an invitation to gang membership. For some, doing so may be a family and neighborhood tradition. Jankowski's second recruitment category is *obligation to community:* "Grandpa was in the gang, I, your poppa, your brother, your two cousins. You're in this family, this hood . . . and, therefore, this gang." Finally, recruitment to membership may be *coercive,* involving pressure of a join-or-else variety: "They have 75 members over there—the West Side has about the same. We only have 40. You want to live here? Join our gang or get your head cracked!"

INITIATION

For some youths, all that need be done to become a member is to accept the invitation to join, whether from acquaintanceship, obligation, or coercion. In gang terms, they "walk in" or are "blessed in." For others, however, severe initiation rites may intervene between invitation and membership. To qualify, the aspiring member may have to fight another member ("the fight in"); undergo a time-limited beating by a group of current members (the "jump in" or "turning in"); commit a serious crime such as a burglary, stealing from a store, a street mugging, or a murder (the "job in"); drink a large quantity of alcohol (the "drink in"); walk through rival gang territory wearing one's own gang's colors (the "mission in"), or physically injure oneself (the "wound in," e.g., shooting oneself in the foot). Females may be required to engage in sexual intercourse with many or all of the members of a companion male gang (the "sex in").

A number of years ago, using groups of several different kinds, we and others demonstrated that the more severe one's initiation into a group, the more attractive membership in it becomes (Aronson & Mills, 1959; Goldstein, 1971). In a sense, the person says, "If I am going through all this, it must really be a very special group." No doubt, severity of gang initiation accounts at least in part for the intense value members often place upon gang membership.

In school settings, gang initiations have in fact taken place in restrooms, in hallways between and during classes, during physical education classes, in school yards, and in those less well-supervised school locations in which nongang student violence also occurs.

TYPES OF MEMBERS

As we noted in the introduction, for some youths gang member-ship is long term, without interruption, and the central fact in their lives. For others, it may be brief, transitory, episodic, and peripheral. For yet others, membership plays out in a manner intermediate to these extremes. Since there are many types of gangs, there are, correspondingly, many types of gang members. While many gang lexicons exist, and many terms apply only to a specific geographic area, the following typology generally reflects the degree of gang involvement.

Hard core or "regulars." These are the youths most central to the gang's existence and functioning. They have been members the longest, are the most active in living out the role of member, and tend to be older than the other members. Often they are the more lethally violent, and their violence is typically employed for material gain. They usually make up no more than half of the typical youth gang.

Peripherals. These youths are more or less part-time, fringe, or associate gang members. They are a part of some gang activities and not others, either at their own choosing or that of the gang at large. Their peripheral membership may last weeks or months, or it can extend over a period of years.

Wannabes. These are most often younger males or females aspiring to regular membership. They are frequently the newcomers to the gang, experimenting with membership. In the process of "earning their rep," they tend to be less lethally violent, and their violence is most often directed toward reputation building.

Potentials. Youngsters living in the gang's neighborhood, known to and by gang members, thought well of by them, but having no commerce with the gang are potential members. If recruited, a portion will decide to accept membership in the gang.

Neutrons. Even in most gang-infested neighborhoods in the United States, the majority of youths, typically 90%, do not belong to a gang (Knox, 1991). Unlike potentials, most neutrons will not join even if a welcoming hand is extended to them. Yet because they live in the gang's neighborhood, rival gang members may suspect that they are in a gang, label them as gang members, and proceed to harass them accordingly. For purposes of self-protection, these youths, too, may come to find gang membership appealing and even necessary.

Veterans. These are older individuals who, after lengthy periods of gang membership, have aged-out, jobbed-out, married-out, or otherwise outgrown their youth gang membership. They may participate on special occasions, such as important celebrations or major fights.

CODES REGULATING MEMBER BEHAVIOR

As is true for any organization, gangs have rules governing member behaviors. Such rules may be formal, codified, and seriously enforced, or they may be unspoken, vague, or situational (i.e., functioning as "but sometime" guides to actions and activities). As Jankowski (1991) has demonstrated, these codes may address a wide variety of expected and desired behavioral prescriptions.

Conflict behavior. Gang violence, defined here as aggression toward person or property outside of the gang, is examined in chapter 5. Gangs' behavioral specifications regarding aggression within the gang typically demand that it be conducted hand-to-hand, without employing weapons. In actuality, within-gang aggression is verbal 85% of the time and involves fighting in only 15% of instances (Goldstein, Glick, Carthan, & Blancero, 1994).

Personal relations. Gangs not infrequently prohibit their members from engaging in romantic relations with the relatives or lovers of other members. Severe, often physical, punishment may follow from violation of this rule.

Consumption of drugs and alcohol. Youth gangs appear to vary widely in this regard. For many, some and even unlimited substance use is the norm. A minority avoid most such behavior, largely to maintain their business-oriented priorities.

Leadership. Gangs are very diverse with regard to leadership. Some have a single leader. Others have a changing number of leaders, varying with the activity being pursued. Others are essentially leaderless. Except in the last instance, gang leadership rules may concern leader selection, leadership change procedures, and the definition of and response to leader abuse of power.

Dress codes. With a degree of rigor and specification paralleling school dress codes, many gangs dictate what their members must wear and how such items are to be worn. Often the items of dress chosen are those explicitly or implicitly proscribed by the school. As Jankowski (1991) has noted:

> The primary objective of most of the [gang] dress codes . . .
> [is] to use clothing to establish a collective identity. Clothing,
> through the medium of the dress code, assume[s] the
> symbolic role of a uniform. It act[s] to identify those
> wearing such clothing with a certain group. (p. 84)

PARENT ROLES

It is clearly easier (though sometimes not that easy) to keep one's child from joining a gang in the first place than it is to extract him or her from such membership once it has begun. School personnel can and should sensitize parents to this possibility when it is suspected. Whenever gang membership is suspected, it is highly desirable that home and school seek to collaborate in the anti-gang effort. (See Figures 24 and 25 in chapter 2 for sample letters used in school-to-home communication.)

What subtle and not-so-subtle warning signs of impending or existing gang membership should be highlighted for parents? Several of those suggested are as follows:

1. The presence of gang graffiti on school books, clothing, or elsewhere

2. Buying or asking the parent to buy an unusual amount of red or blue clothing

3. Wearing or wanting an unusual amount of gold jewelry

4. Staying out later than usual

5. Associating with known or suspected gang members

6. Use of hand signs

7. Possessing unusually large amounts of money

8. Tattoos, patterned burns, clothing, or other items with gang symbols

9. Beginning or increased use of alcohol or drugs

10. Possession of a weapon

SUMMARY

In this chapter we have examined the process of "joining up." We have described which types of youths are prone to gang affiliation, ways they are recruited and initiated, categories of membership, and, as exist in most youth groups, their codes of member behavior. Perhaps most striking is the similarity in motivations for gang membership and for membership in most other, nongang adolescent groups. Youths join gangs to satisfy legitimate needs as well as antisocial desires. These legitimate needs may be met for many youths by prosocial community resources. Addressing prosocial needs rather than the antisocial behaviors that so often characterize gang participation should be the focus of any prevention program.

CHAPTER FOUR

Ethnic Gangs

The arrival of large numbers of European immigrants to eastern seaboard cities in the late 1800s and early 1900s heralded the beginning of the rich social mix that is 20th Century America. During that time, Mexican immigrants arrived and settled in the Southwest, with dramatic increases in the 1920s through the 1940s. In the mid-1940s through the 1950s, large numbers of African Americans migrated internally from the South to the West and Midwest. More recently, immigration from Asia, Southeast Asia, Africa, the Pacific Islands, and elsewhere began in the period from 1965 through 1975 and has continued on into the present. During each of these waves of immigration, gangs have developed and grown. Native Americans, residents of this country long before these waves of immigration, have found gangs in their midst only recently.

Newly arrived immigrants then, as today, often clustered in ethnic neighborhoods, seeking the familiarity and advantages of common language, culture, social norms, and social structures (e.g., churches, schools, settlement houses). Internal migrations also occurred, with the resettlement of ethnic groups, especially African Americans from the deep South to the industrial job centers of the Midwest and Southern California. Whether of European, Asian, African, or Hispanic/Latino descent, foreign-born immigrants and internal migrants encountered strong opposing forces along with the promise of a new life. The advantages of seeking sameness were generally accompanied by the disadvantages of being perceived and received as new, different, and often threatening to those who had arrived before. As these newly arrived persons began competing for jobs, housing, and social resources, established former immigrants commonly opposed the newcomers. This attempt to gain or retain control over resources, rather than to grant access to those newly arrived, is little different today than in years past. Recently, immigrants from Eastern Europe, Southeast Asia, and Somalia have been similarly stigmatized.

The European gangs of the late 19th and early 20th centuries (including the Irish gangs of Boston and New York, the Polish and other Eastern European gangs of New York, and the Jewish gangs of New York and Detroit) formed partly as a response to a perceived need for protection, self-defense, economic gain, and recreation. All such gangs were ultimately destructive to their communities and to the individuals who joined them. This is true irrespective of the needs or desires the gangs originally fulfilled. Then as now, these early gangs represented a small percentage of marginalized youth, living among an already marginalized population of immigrants. Gangs have waxed and waned over the decades, some disappearing completely, some evolving into adult organized criminal enterprises, and some continuing little changed to this day.

SOME CAUTIONARY COMMENTS

It should be apparent that, however broadly or narrowly one separates people into groups, defined by the groups themselves or by others, the number of gangs, the course of their development and evolution, and the particulars of their unique gang subcultures will differ. This chapter focuses on the major ethnic gangs in the U.S. today: those whose members are primarily of European, African, Hispanic/Latino, Asian, and Native American descent. However, one could easily and with great interest observe and comment on the development of less well-known ethnic gangs, such as those with members of Samoan, Tongan, Philippine, Somali, or other origin.

When discussing ethnic gangs, it is imperative to do so cautiously. From observations of specific cultural differences across ethnic gangs, it is possible to make the unwarranted assumption that some intrinsic aspect of an ethnic group is responsible for the development of gangs within that culture. Instead, it is the disorganizing stresses of life common to all people that act upon youth and social structures within ethnic communities to create and maintain youth gang subcultures. These stresses—as well as discrimination, economic and social marginalization, and the development of an urban and, increasingly, rural underclass—interact with intrapersonal variables to create and maintain youth gangs.

William Julius Wilson (1991) notes that core concentrations of poverty (i.e., areas with greater than 40% of residents living below the poverty line) occur primarily within communities of color (i.e., ethnic communities). Poverty, job loss to suburbs, outmigration, and an accompanying loss of social support structures have left a dearth of conventional, prosocial individuals, families, and institutions to support the development of youth. The loss of these positive, community-building assets often leads to gang formation.

Wilson maintains that youth who grow up in neighborhoods where families have a steady breadwinner will "tend to develop some of the disciplined habits associated with stable or steady employment," behaviors that are coherent and ordered and that provide the "anchor for the temporal and spatial aspects of daily life" (p. 10). These behaviors also can be assumed to be the underpinnings of school success. Social disorganization amidst poverty provides the marginalizing conditions that interfere with the development of self-efficacy and self-determination for youth. Impoverished youth often perceive a certain randomness to the relation between their behavior and social or economic gain. These nonresilient youth, with access to few of the assets known to immunize children against negative living conditions, often experience despair. Striving to gain or exhibit skills to produce social, school, and economic success appears irrelevant to youth living in jobless poverty and social disorganization. To put this idea more strongly, when guns are firing outside the window, doing one's homework can seem insignificant.

When concentrations of jobless, poor families occur (i.e., when ghettos form), social disorganization is common, leaving youth amenable to available social organizing forces. These forces often include gangs or other delinquent groups. Gang role models—ever present in music, literature, video, and film—also contribute to gang formation and evolution.

Even in such disenfranchised communities, from the heart of large urban areas to the isolated Native American reservations of the Midwest and West, most youth do not engage in delinquent or gang behavior. Gang youth typically represent no more than 3 to 10% of age-eligible youth in any given community. Rarely are well-substantiated figures higher than 7 to 10% of the age-eligible population of 11- to 21-year-old youth (Spergel, 1990).

This observation should clarify that nothing about ethnic communities per se is gang engendering. Social, economic, and intrapersonal variables interact to make individuals prone to joining gangs. These social, structural, cultural, and individual variables interact to produce and maintain gangs within ethnic communities. Youth gang members commonly cloak themselves in selected trappings of their ethnic culture. Specific cultural variables then interact within the specific context of a given community to create specific ethnic gang differences.

What differences, then, are ethnic differences? Research is clear that the differences among ethnic gangs are far less significant than are the similarities. Stated otherwise, the character of gang-related behavior across gangs is a far greater commonality than is the ethnic character of each gang. Nonetheless, compelling reasons remain to discuss ethnic differences across gangs. Prevention and intervention can take place only within the cultural context of the affected community. Years of mistrust, disappointment, and marginalization make a basic understanding of cultural concepts within ethnic communities imperative. It is also imperative to know and understand the perceptions of community members about the specific problems caused by the gang-involved youth who live in those neighborhoods.

Cultural stereotypes are characterized by total uniformity of opinion, little variability, and a narrow range of behavior. However, within a given ethnic community there is a wide range of opinion as to what one's ethnicity means and as to what constitutes a culturally acceptable or even culturally specific prevention or intervention strategy. Indeed, there is often a range of opinion as to whether or not gangs are a significant problem in themselves or a rational, albeit troublesome, response to racism and discrimination. A lack of flexibility in response, a rigid construct of racial-ethnic issues, or a mindset closed to a broad range of cultural attitudes, expectations, and behaviors will certainly doom interventions to failure and to rejection by the individuals and communities one most wishes to serve.

With such caveats in mind, the following description of existing and prototypical ethnic gang structures is intended to help educators plan effective prevention, intervention, and emergency response procedures in their schools. Such efforts are essential to create a safe campus, promote social and academic growth for students, and develop and maintain a strong connection between school and community.

EUROPEAN AMERICAN GANGS

Early immigrants to New York, Boston, and Philadelphia saw the development of youth gangs among early white immigrants, especially those from Ireland, as early as the 1800s. Detroit's notorious Purple Gang of the early 1900s was formed among middle-class youth from the Jewish community. They quickly evolved into a broad-ranging organized criminal gang of adults, dissolving in the 1940s (Bak, 1992).

Spergel (1990) reviews the onset of European American immi-grant gangs in New York, while Klein (1995) notes that prior to the middle of the century, youth gangs in the larger cities were primarily white, including youngsters of Irish, Polish, and Italian descent. Some of these gangs evolved into ongoing criminal enterprises, some dissolved as each ethnic group assimilated into the cultural main-stream, and yet others continue more-or-less the same to this day. Membership in some Irish American and European American street gangs is a rite of passage for a subset of youth until young adulthood, at which time the gang member continues some social affiliation but generally ceases criminal gang activity. Other contemporary white street gangs include such groups as the Chicago-based Simon City Royals and Gaylords. These and other exclusively white gangs commonly adopt the signs and symbols of other street gangs in the city where they exist, modifying the symbols to gain specific recog-nition. The Midwest has recently seen the development of other white gangs adopting the language, dress, symbols, and behavior of African American and Hispanic/Latino gangs. Such exclusively white gangs appear in cities both large and small, and increasingly in small towns and rural areas.

Rarely does a white gang invite membership from peers of color, while other ethnic groups sometimes invite white participation, gen-erally as a function of the young affiliates' having grown up with or attended school with the core ethnic gang members. Nonetheless, white gangs are generally exclusively white, with members usually drawn from the immediate neighborhood, a single school, or the community and commonly being known to one another before the gang's formation. They may be primarily deviant play groups, en-gaging in a restricted range of delinquent behavior, including minor consumption of alcohol, fighting, and petty theft, or they may engage in a broader and more serious range of crimes against persons, up to and including homicide.

The prevalence of white gangs is approximately 1 to 5% of age-eligible youth in an affected community (Howell, 1996d). White gangs are more likely to engage primarily in property crimes than are African American or Hispanic/Latino gangs. Specialization, such as drug trafficking, is not apparent. Where present, white street gangs will use hand signs, often display gang tattoos and gang jewelry, and engage in graffiti vandalism.

Tagger Crews

Tagger crews, primarily white youth who engage exclusively in costly and destructive graffiti vandalism, are sometimes viewed as youth gangs but do not exhibit any other common attributes of youth gangs. While there is concern that such groups are becoming increasingly violent, only time will tell if they will evolve into more typical youth gangs. The main activity of tagger crews is moving through a community, quietly and without detection, placing their identifying graffiti (i.e., their nicknames, ranging from modest letter-ing in pen to large, multicolored murals) on walls, buildings, or vehicles. Taggers are the antithesis of gangs in that they are often solitary, exhibit few identifiers, seek to avoid direct confrontation with rival taggers or tagger crews, and have a very limited range of delinquent or criminal behavior.

Ideological or Single-Issue Gangs

Ideological, or single-issue, white gangs are not strictly street gangs in that they generally do not engage in "cafeteria-style" crimes (i.e., a range of diverse crimes, including property crimes, drug crimes, and crimes against persons). Nonetheless, such groups typically have a common name, use some public symbols, have a known presence in the community, and endure over time. They may sport tattoos but only rarely display hand signs, create identity graffiti, and claim turf. Despite their lack of primary street gang attributes, they represent a clear and present danger in many communities. In schools, ideological gangs that support racial segregation, race hate, or exclusive, whites-only ideology may cause social disorder directly by verbally or physically attacking students of color and/or by vandalizing the school and community with white-power slogans. The indirect effect of such gangs on persons of color is also apparent. White supremacist groups, however large or small in a given school, may polarize constituencies within the school, destabilize the school community, and drive frightened or angry youth of color out of the school or into self-defense groups or "near-gangs." While the prevalence of white street gangs in the general adolescent population is stable or on the decline, some ad hoc and ongoing ideological, "whites-only" gangs appear to be on the increase across the country.

The youth attracted to whites-only street gangs (i.e., those gangs that engage in a typically broad range of criminal behavior) are often similar to their ethnic peers along personal, social, economic, and educational variables. Although they generally do not experience racial marginalization, such youth are typically distinct along other critical variables, including early history of behavior problems and academic deficiencies as well as emphasis on physical prowess and preference for physical dispute resolution. Such youths also tend to come from low-income distressed families, often with an absent father; often live in neighborhoods marked by social disorganization and poor parental supervision or involvement; and sometimes live in neighborhoods that have a number of role model or rival gang members directly in the neighborhood, attending the school, or living immediately adjacent to the neighborhood. White gang members are therefore marginal within their own adolescent and greater community.

Recently, with the seemingly omnipresent media images of ethnic "gangster chic" in clothing, language, music, and video, it has become acceptable and even desirable for some white youths to imitate and aspire to gangster status. In suburban and rural communities, imitation has resulted in exclusively white gangs, largely comprised of troubled and troubling youth. Such youth find that to assume the persona of urban ethnic gang members is to gain a certain power they might otherwise fail to receive. Rarely do such youth have any real contacts with urban ethnic gangsters. They may, however, engage in a significant range of antisocial and criminal behavior.

Members of exclusive, whites-only urban youth gangs present many of the same social problems to the community as do their ethnic peers. The pattern of their antisocial behaviors will vary over time but will generally mimic that of their ethnic peers living in adjacent areas. Specifically, such gangs will develop their own history and rules regarding drug use, range of violent and other criminal behaviors, and specific relationship to the conventional structures of the community from which they arise. Intervention is likely to be effective to the degree that close supervision, prosocial skill acquisition, and increased parental involvement occur. The absence of the severe social stresses common in pockets of urban or rural poverty likely accounts for the low percentage of gang involvement by white youths. This low probability of involvement should make individual and community response to white gangs promising.

Effective prevention and intervention programs with white gang members must reflect sensitivity to gang type: traditional single-ethnic street gang, mixed-ethnic street gang, other single-issue gang (e.g., white supremacist), or single-issue instrumental or business gang (e.g., drug gang). Next the functional context in which the gang has developed must be assessed. Is the gang a defensive response to a real or perceived threat, such as from another gang of the same or a different ethnic group? Is the gang a delinquent play group; a business venture; a status, turf, or social control group; a visible expression of racial discord in the school or community; or a traditional street gang involved in cafeteria-style crime? Effective, proportional responses can occur only if the initial assessment of the situation is carefully conducted. Not all gangs are alike, even within a given school or neighborhood. More will be said about how to conduct such an assessment and how to develop prevention and intervention strategies in chapter 6.

AFRICAN AMERICAN GANGS

African American gangs evolved primarily in the heart of the Midwest states and concurrently in Southern California. Southern rural families moved north and west around the time of World War II to seek employment in the industrial belt of the Midwest and the new industries of California. While gainful, living-wage employment allowed many rural and poor families to move into the middle-class mainstream of some cities, discriminatory policies in housing, along with job availability in central cities, contributed to high concentrations of African Americans in small geographic areas. As the newly prosperous African American middle class began to move their families and personal and economic assets from these neighborhoods to other areas and cities, unrelated decreases in industrial employment opportunities occurred. The industrial belt became the rust belt, and economic gains for African Americans slid steeply down (Lemann, 1986a, 1986b; Wilson, 1991). The loss of living-wage jobs combined with the loss of social capital resulting from the outmigration of many members of the middle class, discriminatory housing policies, and the civil unrest of the late 1950s and early 1960s to produce conditions ripe for gang development.

As industry jobs declined or disappeared altogether, many families became further marginalized by race, social customs, income, neighborhood disorganization, and, ultimately, family dissolution in the face of chronic joblessness. Street gangs in this population first appeared in the large industrial areas of the Midwest and California.

Concurrently, the civil rights movement began, publicly highlighting the destabilizing and discriminatory forces that had always faced African American families. While most moved forward in a prosocial manner amidst the chaos, some youth and young adults gathered in social groups that evolved into the current "supergangs" of the Midwest: the Disciples and Vice Lords. Chicago-style gangs are present in various forms in 35 states (Howell, 1996c). The concurrent evolution of the supergangs of the West Coast followed a somewhat different course, nonetheless resulting in the Los Angeles–style gangs identified as Crips or Bloods. Present in 42 states, the LA-style supergangs, some closely but most only loosely affiliated, allegedly controlled almost 35% of the crack cocaine trade in the 1980s (Howell, 1996d).

Ethnicity and Antisocial Behavior

African American street gangs represent 48 to 49% of all gang members (Howell, 1996d). Such figures are deeply disturbing and easily misinterpreted to suggest that there is something intrinsic to African American culture that causes gang behavior. Nothing could be further from the truth. African American communities have a higher percentage of gang members than other ethnic groups for simple, if tragic, reasons. Many African American youth, along with others physically identifiable as members of ethnic groups, are visible within the greater community and therefore subject to housing, employment, and social discrimination. In addition, they suffer a higher rate of multiple generations living in poverty and more frequently live in socially disorganized, unstable neighborhoods, in households with an absent father, and in neighborhoods in which gangs have existed long before they themselves are of age to join. Clearly, these conditions marginalize many African American youth, who are already suspect in the eyes of many in society at large. What is most striking is not that so many youths living under such conditions are gang members, but that so many are not. Even in highly gang-impacted neighborhoods, perhaps 15 to 20% of age-eligible youth claim gang affiliation; this means 80 to 85% stay out of the gang (Spergel, 1990). Social conditions, not genes, create gangs.

Having said all this, we caution the reader that understandable reasons are not justifications for joining a gang. African American youth gangs often find willing and knowledgeable, or unwitting, adults in the community who defend the gang members as "good kids" who just hang around and occasionally get into trouble, "just like any kids." Adults sometimes benefit directly or indirectly from the gang presence and may defend gang youth against what they view as the greater threat of racist labeling and oppression. Indeed, in the history of African American gangs, it has not been uncommon for some social service providers who work with antisocial youth to find themselves defending the involvement of youth in street gangs (Spergel, 1990). Other defenders include gang apologists, adult gang leaders who present themselves as de facto youth leaders, and otherwise decent citizens who have tired of racist attitudes toward neighborhood youth. Gang-involved youth, like any others, commonly wrap themselves in their adult defenders' excuses and protective statements. The best intentions of well-meaning adults often go awry, actually maintaining the gang presence in the community. Looking on the gang as legitimate (i.e., an acceptable social substructure within a school or community) will only hasten school or community destabilization. Irrespective of the understandable reasons for a high prevalence of gang membership among African American youth, the cost of such membership for individual youths and their communities is severe.

African American gang members are more involved in drug trafficking than are other gangs that specialize in the drug trade (Howell, 1996a, 1996c). This is consistent with the shocking finding of Stanton and Galbraith (1994) that nearly 9% of a sample of urban African American youth admitted to drug trafficking.

While gang homicides occur within and across all ethnic gangs, they are slightly less frequent among African American gangs than among Hispanic/Latino gangs, even when neighborhood variables are held constant. However, the rate of nongang homicides among African Americans is higher in comparison to other ethnic groups, with chronic, long-term poverty being the likely relevant variable

(Curry & Spergel, 1988). These attributes can and do vary over time, depending upon numerous community variables. Some African American gangs have high rates of interethnic gang homicide. Others engage in short-lived but bloody shooting-retaliation-shooting cycles. In Chicago, African American gang–related homicides versus non-gang-related homicides have risen dramatically since 1990, perhaps as a result of increasing involvement in the drug trade (Bell & Jenkins, 1990; Howell, 1996b, 1996c).

Gang Prototypes

African American youth who claim gang membership generally represent themselves as members or affiliates of one of four major gang prototypes: Vice Lords or "People," a Chicago-based gang with hierarchical leadership and representation in 35 states; Disciples or "Folks," a second Chicago-based gang; Crips, a Los Angeles–based gang; or Bloods, a second Los Angeles–based gang. Within each of these gangs are smaller subunits, generally referred to as *sets* but sometimes as *cliques, crews,* or *posses.* These terms will vary across cities and sometimes within cities. Each gang unit is generally small, with 12 to 25 members, generally within a small age-distribution band—for example, 12- to 18-year-old males. Usually, sets are exclusively male and African American, but occasionally they include other youth, typically from the same school, block, or neighborhood. A gang set may or may not be affiliated with older, adult gang members. In cities where the gang is in the early stages of evolution, there may be little adult leadership. In cities with an evolving and mature gang problem, both independent youth sets and adult-directed, highly structured gangs are present. Members of such gangs occupy specific, defined roles in the gang, with titles or rank, a tightly or loosely defined chain of command, and written rules and codes of conduct. New members generally must swear allegiance to the code of conduct.

Joining the Gang

As with most ethnic gangs, African American youth generally become introduced to the gang through simple proximity. Nongang youth may meet gang members at school, parties, recreation centers, and city parks. Usually, they associate for the same reasons any other youth form affinity groups (i.e., for friendship, recreation, access to girls, sports, and so forth). Sometimes individuals begin their association because they are impressed with the perceived power and status of the gang, because they fear abuse from other gangs in the school or neighborhood, and occasionally for specific business reasons. The offer to join the gang is often casual and open-ended, and the potential member has time for consideration. Less commonly, active gang members will approach and directly recruit the potential member. Irrespective of the approach, refusal without consequence may or may not be an option, depending upon the specific gang and their influence in the community. Curry and Spergel (1992) note that African American youth are more likely to join gangs as a function of proximity to or interaction with older gang members—in the family, school, or immediate neighborhood—than as a function of interpersonal variables such as low self-esteem or school stress.

A small number of intergenerational African American gang members are christened into the gang the day of their birth, when a graffiti-emblazoned christening blanket is laid on the crib and photos are taken of the gang-involved parents as they hold weapons or display gang hand signs over the baby. The vast majority of African American youth who join gangs do so by more pedestrian means at early adolescence, typically at the age of 11 to 13 years. A few of these youth are "walked into" or "blessed into" the gang by adults who have personal knowledge of the novice. Such youths need not prove themselves by committing a crime or being beaten by the gang. Less fortunate youth are surrounded by several current gang members, who then beat the new candidate, generally for 20 seconds to a minute. The initiation may occur in a city park, near the youth's residence, on gang turf (for gangs that claim turf), in the school yard, and, occasionally, in a classroom, much to the astonishment of teachers and classmates.

Youth who live in gang-impacted neighborhoods and who allege gang affiliation but who are not recognized as gangsters by local gang members are frequently referred to as "perpetrators" or "wannabes." These terms are often meant to be pejorative, demeaning, or discounting. Individuals younger than age 15 who are recognized by the gang as having gang potential typically are called "shorties" but are sometimes identified as being "jr.s," "babies" or by similar diminutives.

Gang Hierarchy and Conduct

African American gangs are generally hierarchical in nature, as is the case with Hispanic/Latino gangs, which also commonly have an elaborate hierarchical structure. Formal rank with titles and differential responsibility is common in both the Disciples and Vice Lords and, to a lesser degree, the Crips and Bloods. Young gang members, even marginal members, typically know and can recite the gang hierarchy up through the names and rank of adult members serving time in prison.

Written codes or rules of conduct are common in African American gangs. Young members often memorize some or all of the gang code and symbols. In graffiti and in public discussion, the gang is usually referred to as an organization or nation, rarely as a gang. Relating the rules and symbols to various African religions or customs is common in these writings and apparently legitimizes the gang in the eyes of young members.

Signs and Symbols

African American gangs utilize common symbols, with many variations for individual sets. The most common symbols are a six-point star, a heart with wings of flame, and upright pitchforks for the

Disciples, and a five-point star, top hat and cane, and Playboy bunny for the Vice Lords. Bloods and Crips generally forsake such symbolism for coded alphabet lettering and the words *Crip* or *Blood*. Disciples and, to a greater extent, Vice Lords will use coded alphabets and the many subsymbols for the gang.

Tagging of neighborhoods, schools, notebooks, school lockers, desks, tables, and virtually anything that doesn't move with gang graffiti is common. Tattoos are common in African American gangs, either self-administered "kitchen table" or "jailhouse" efforts or more formal semiprofessional or professional work. Tattoos generally depict the basic gang symbols as well as gang nicknames. Careful attention to gang graffiti therefore will provide school staff and others in the community with a picture of the gang's development.

SPANISH-SPEAKING GANGS

Spanish-speaking people in the United States today reflect a broad range of historical, cultural, and racial differences. It is important to stress, then, that Spanish-speaking gangs are not a monolithic group; rather, they reflect the diversity of the various Spanish-speaking communities from which they arise. Nomenclature of Spanish-speaking gangs can become a problem for persons attempting to work with gang-involved youngsters. Gangs in the Eastern and Southeastern parts of this country may be of primarily Puerto Rican descent and thus refer to themselves as Puerto Rican gangs. Gangs composed mostly of youth of Caribbean or Central American descent generally identify themselves as Latino gangs. Southwestern and Western gangs may refer to themselves as Chicano/Latino or Mexican. In the Midwest, the terms Hispanic, Mexican, Latino, and Chicano/Latino all may be employed by different gangs and by different community members in referring to gang members, making it difficult for educators to address a specific gang-impacted, Spanish-speaking community respectfully. To avoid inaccurate characterizations, it is important to listen carefully to how community members publicly refer to themselves.

At present, youth in the dominant Spanish-speaking gangs in this country are of Mexican, Puerto Rican, Central American, Caribbean, or Latino descent. Where a specific group is meant, we will use the specific term employed by that group (e.g., *Chicano*). When information pertains to Spanish-speaking gangs more generally, we will use either that designation or the term *Hispanic/Latino.*

Gang Characteristics

Spanish-speaking gangs make up 28 to 43% of the nation's street gangs, depending on the study characteristics and definitions (e.g., including all major Spanish-speaking groups or distinguishing such demographic categories as "white Spanish-speaking"; Howell, 1996d). Several studies suggest that Hispanic/Latino gangs account for a high proportion of gang homicides per capita in comparison to other ethnic gangs and are involved in more overall gang violence than other gangs (Howell, 1996b, 1996c). However, nongang homicides among Spanish-speaking populations are comparatively low and similar to homicides in white populations (Curry & Spergel, 1988). Curry and Spergel (1992) further suggest that geographic migration, combined with high social disorganization, is a major causal variable in gang homicides within areas occupied by Spanish-speaking gangs.

While individual Spanish-speaking youths join gangs for the same range of reasons as other youth, as a group such youths are more likely to join for interpersonal reasons (e.g., low self-esteem, poor attachment to school, school failure) than are other ethnic youth (Curry & Spergel, 1992). Traditionally, the membership of Hispanic/Latino gangs is large, with many smaller age-graded sets, or *palomillas.* The Spanish-speaking gang may use the term *clique* or *crew* to describe the basic unit. The larger groups are commonly territorial or turf-based, involve the participation of members ranging widely in age, and often persist in a community over generations.

However, the length of an individual member's tenure with the gang is often shorter than for other ethnic groups (Curry & Spergel, 1988).

Gang structure is often but not always hierarchical, with a defined leader. Graffiti symbolism generally consists of nicknames, letters indicating the gang name, and numbers—often the street numbers defining the turf boundary. In Mexican American gangs, especially those of the West Coast, the stereotypical, stylized image of a Mexican gang member, the face of a clown, or the happy and sad harlequins of the theater are incorporated in tattoos or graffiti. The imagery of the tears of a clown, symbolizing the fatalism of a "live today, die tomorrow" attitude, is common. Melancholy images of Spanish-speaking gang life are popular with both younger and older gang members.

Elaborate script, often with the appearance of Old English, is common in gang writings, graffiti, and tattoos. Memorial walls are often created in alleys or behind public buildings. Most are a few square yards, but some cover 50 or more square yards. On the walls will be the names of deceased gang members, portraits of crying clowns, and perhaps a roster of gang members' names. Researchers cite the importance of the concepts of *machismo* (physical prowess), *locura* (craziness), and family—particularly the gang as second, chosen family—in explaining the general violence within these gangs (Vigil, 1990). Resignation, melancholy, a "seize the day" attitude, and pride in physical prowess characterize the range of Spanish-speaking gangs across the United States.

Many Spanish-speaking gangs are now well into their fifth generation in population centers in California (especially Los Angeles and San Diego), Texas, Arizona, and elsewhere. Chicago and New York also have several multigenerational, Spanish-speaking gangs. Gangs such as the Eighteenth Street of California and the Latin Kings of New York and Chicago have captured the attention of both gang researchers and the media, making them known and frequently emulated by impressionable youth who live far beyond these gangs' geographic boundaries. Through the media and through the migration of other Spanish-speaking peoples to the same or adjacent neighborhoods, the prototypical Mexican American gangster persona has spread. Mexican American gangs are next examined in detail, as they have come to represent the archetype for all Spanish-speaking gangs.

Mexican American Gangs

The Mexican American culture of the California coast evolved in cities and rural areas of the state with little observable gang presence until about World War II. While some authors trace the arrival of gangs to the Southwest following the Mexican revolution of 1813, the convergence of sociopolitical forces during World War II is seen by most as the beginning of present-day Mexican American gangs (Appier, 1990; Moore, 1991). Delinquent gangs were surely present in some form prior to this time but were given little public notice.

A number of factors set the stage for gang formation and, more important, gang evolution: public opinion, polarizing social conditions characteristic during the upheaval of wartime, and the stress of too few and unqualified "special police" and probation officers to replace those regular-duty officers who had gone to war. In addition, the mass internal migration of many ethnic groups to California to work in the war industries, as well as the public positions taken by some elected officials and the media, caused intense marginalizing forces to emerge within the Mexican American community (Appier, 1990; Moore, 1983, 1991; Moore, Vigil, & Garcia, 1983; Vigil, 1983, 1990). The tragic "Zoot Suit" riots of the early 1940s were a reflection of this enormous and violent social unrest and aggression toward Mexican Americans. Whites, often servicemen, attacked Mexican American youth and adults, who were perceived as threatening simply by their presence or dress (i.e., their stylized Zoot suits). It is ironic to note that the Zoot suit style was itself copied from the nightclub dress common in New York's Harlem neighborhood.

These forces, extreme exacerbations of preexisting conditions in the Mexican American community, brought together nondelinquent youth in self-defense groups, galvanized groups of delinquent youth, and gave focus and purpose to existing gang youth, creating the proto-gangs of that time.

Recently, some formal connection between Mexican American street gangs and the organized crime gangs of Mi Familia and Nuestra Familia have been alleged by law enforcement. It is suggested that some traditional street gangs have been employed to transport drugs from Mexico to the United States. While overall the linkage between street gangs and the drug trade is weak, the possibility of greater linkage for a given gang in a given neighborhood or city is significant. In some cities, street gangs control or at least participate to a great degree in the drug trade (Howell, 1996a).

ASIAN AMERICAN GANGS

Few ethnic gangs are so steeped in folklore as are Asian American gangs. While the range of Asian cultures in this country is broad and diverse, most Americans associate youth of Chinese and ethnic Chinese-Vietnamese national descent with Asian gangs. Indeed, images are firmly implanted of gangs associated with the Chinese Tongs—family and benevolent associations of the 1800s railroad era of the West Coast and, to some extent, New York City. Such Tong-based gangs were the strong arm of these family associations and fought for control of the Chinatowns of the West.

Presently, dominant gangs are, ethnically, Chinese or Southeast Asian. The main Southeast Asian gangs include youth of Vietnamese, Hmong, Lao, and Cambodian descent.

Chinese American Gangs

The Chinese Exclusion Act of 1882 greatly slowed the growth of Chinese immigration in North America for almost 50 years. The repeal in 1943 of this act increased the total number of Chinese immigrants in the now rapidly growing Chinatowns of the U.S. New Chinese immigrants, mainly Cantonese, began to arrive in great numbers, destabilizing the delicate social balance of largely segregated communities of Chinese nationals and Chinese Americans in the United States and Canada.

Gangs among Chinese American youth did not become a visible presence in the greater community until the 1960s, partially as the result of the easing of immigration policies. At that time there was a rapid influx of Chinese nationals seeking the promise of this country's "Gold Mountain" (i.e., a better life in America, especially California). Beginning around 1965, these new arrivals, often teens and young men from greater Canton and Hong Kong, were viewed as marginal even within the Chinatowns of the U.S. and Canada. Community-based Chinese settlement houses and other social service agencies were insufficient to assist the new immigrants. Many young men became disenfranchised and desperate in already isolated and highly controlled communities. Soon many of them formed typical street gangs, but with a twist: These gangs formed associations with criminally inclined adult members of certain modern-day Tongs. While the main purpose of these family associations is to provide social, business, and community contacts within communities with large Chinese and Chinese American populations, some members with criminal interests sought out, employed, or sheltered the newly formed gangs, each meeting the economic needs of the other. Gangs provided protection for gambling houses, prostitution, and collection rackets, which preyed on small businesses and restaurants. The arrival of many Chinese-Vietnamese youth following the fall of Saigon in 1975 increased the number of Asian-born youth into new and traditional enclaves of Chinese and Vietnamese-Chinese families, further destabilizing these neighborhoods (Chin, 1990, 1996; Joe & Robinson, 1980; Kodluboy, 1997).

Today, Chinese American gangs take the form of traditional youth/street gangs with little adult involvement, street gangs closely associated with members of the family associations (especially those who support illegal gambling houses), and gangs associated with the largely criminal Triads of Hong Kong (Chin, 1990, 1996). The Triads initially formed over 600 years ago as part of a political resistance movement in mainland China. Law enforcement authorities around the world presently view the Triads primarily as organized criminal enterprises. As Chin (1996) notes, reasons these youths join gangs include monetary gain, protection from other predatory youth, recreation, brotherhood (i.e., "family"), and power.

Southeast Asian–American Gangs

Southeast Asian–American gangs, primarily youths of Vietnamese, Hmong, Lao, and Cambodian descent, are a comparatively new phenomenon in this country, having their onset after 1975 with the end of the Vietnam Conflict and the resultant exodus of immigrants fleeing the advancing communist armies. Many of the new arrivals, often refugees from Thailand or Vietnam, were survivors of the political purges of Laos, Cambodia, and Vietnam. Some affluent, well-educated, and politically connected refugees came relatively directly to the U.S. Others, less fortunate, languished for years in the refugee border camps of Thailand, where they awaited resettlement and where some immigrants wait even today.

Within these diverse communities are immigrants of widely varying circumstance. Across each community are equally widely varying social customs and histories. Some Southeast Asian ethnic enclaves, often referred to as Chinatowns, are now better viewed as "Asia-towns," where primarily Southeast Asian, rather than Chinese, immigrants have established their economies. Each Southeast Asian culture is rich and varied. Regrettably, some educators and others do not differentiate among these groups; however, the gangs that have formed within each culture have their own unique ethnic characteristics.

Vietnamese American Gangs

Vietnamese American street gangs are quite commonly comprised of older youth and young adults, typically have some connection with criminal adults in the community, and are often ethnic Chinese. These gangs engage in a wide variety of crimes and have little interaction with other gang members of Southeast Asian descent. Indeed, Vietnamese gang members view themselves as the elite of Asian gangs.

Quick, successive waves of immigration from Vietnam reflected differing family types. Initially, the arrivals were well-educated and financially strong, intact families. These first-wave immigrants were, as a result of the invasion of then South Vietnam, quickly followed by poor, non-English-speaking refugee families. It is among the later immigrants (i.e., those most highly marginalized by circumstance) that most gangs arose. Vietnamese gangs are found even in cities where relatively small numbers of such youth are present. These gangs first specialized in home invasion robberies, car thefts, and extortion of Asian businesses and have evolved to include elaborate, multijurisdictional financial fraud activities.

Among Vietnamese American gangs, graffiti vandalism is uncommon; when it does occur, the graffiti sometimes follow the patterns of other ethnic gangs but are more typically limited to the gangs' initials. Tattoos are similar in design and placement to those of other ethnic gangs and may also include culturally specific nongang images such as tigers, eagles, or dragons. Gang dress often is stylized gangster chic and frequently not a useful identifier, as the manner of dress changes relatively quickly.

Gang "representing" (i.e., identifying oneself as a gang member) on the school campus is uncommon. When it does occur, it is generally limited to a subdued imitation of the dress of other ethnic gangs in the school community. Some Vietnamese American gang members remain good students throughout high school, all the while concealing their gang identity. Students of Vietnamese descent are often viewed as the "model minority," a somewhat patronizing and subtly racist viewpoint. Because these students are generally quiet and polite to adults, their problems and fears are often overlooked by school personnel.

Increasingly, Vietnamese American gang members follow a less conventional path, adopting gangster chic dress and demeanor, as well as presenting the school with numerous problems of truancy, dropout, poor school performance, and sporadic violence on or near campus. Still, these youth generally do quite well in school, simply because they study more than their peers and because most still have strong traditional family structures. Increasing Americanization and family stresses (e.g., loss of the father's traditional role and resultant family destabilization) are creating more problems within the Vietnamese American community.

Hmong, Lao, and Cambodian American Gangs

Hmong, Lao, and Cambodian immigrants are among the most disenfranchised of the Asian groups. From the 1970s through the present, these groups have come to this country as refugees, often after suffering brutal abuse and the slaughter of family members by communist forces as they fled their homelands. Many families arrived in the U.S. without fathers or older brothers. Many other families found themselves in nontraditional roles in communities that were anything but welcoming. Surviving fathers who were physicians, military leaders, or political figures in their former homelands were forced by language isolation and other circumstance to adopt greatly diminished employment and social roles. The impact of these forces on children has been significant. While most children from these communities quickly assimilate into American culture, a small percentage do not. It is among these youth that most gang members are found.

Originally, gang members of Hmong, Lao, and Cambodian descent formed cross-cultural coalitions. The rationale was to establish a common defense against abusive white youth and African American and Hispanic/Latino gangs, which were already established in the poor and socially disorganized neighborhoods initially settled by Southeast Asian immigrants. With the arrival of more Southeast Asian youth, conflict over access to and control of resources began. Gang members of Hmong, Lao, and Cambodian descent commonly cite racial harassment and assault from other youth, especially from members of other ethnic gangs, as one important reason for their forming youth gangs. With increasing internal migration and immigration from overseas, absolute numbers as well as concentrations of each Southeast Asian group have risen, allowing the groups to split off into generally homogeneous ethnic gangs. At this point, the population of each ethnic group is sufficiently large that gangs within each community now compete among themselves for power, status, and resources.

Each of these ethnic gangs tends to model African American and Hispanic/Latino gangs closely in terms of gang names, dress, hand signs, general interaction, patterns of language, and terms used to describe gang life and activities. Graffiti and tattoos also closely imitate the imagery of other gangs.

Gang rivalries, like those most common to all ethnic gangs, tend to be interethnic. On occasion, violence will erupt across ethnic lines. For example, in 1991, Hispanic/Latino and Cambodian gangs engaged in an intense period of shooting in Long Beach, California (Mydans, 1991). Frequent, low-intensity interethnic violence may occur when the groups encounter one another in the community, but most planned and serious violence and most business and social interactions occur in interethnic dyads. Loose and shifting affiliations, generally across broad Crip and Blood lines, may form. Conflicts may then include two affiliated gangs against two other affiliated gangs.

According to Howell (1996d), youngsters of Southeast Asian descent as a group represent the smallest percentage of gang-involved youth, comprising 4 to 7% of age-eligible youth. Even if they do belong to a gang, these youth commonly perform well, socially and academically, until junior high school age, at which time truancy, delinquent activity, and solidification of the gangster image occur.

Few Asian American youth are involved in criminal activity (Howell, 1996d), and of all incarcerated juveniles of Asian descent, the greatest percentage are active gang members, affiliate closely with gang members, or are members of a family with an active gang member (Kodluboy, 1998). While the popular stereotype is that Asian American gangs are more violent than other ethnic gangs, there appear to be little data to support this perception. Indeed, it is possible the perception that Asian American gang members are disproportionately violent may stem from the fact that whatever violence they do commit is likely to be in a highly public place, to involve relatively large numbers of individuals, and, increasingly, to involve handguns (Kodluboy, 1997).

Another reason for the low level of criminal gang activity among Asian American youths may be that few youth of Southeast Asian descent join gangs. When these youths do join a gang, it reflects a significant break from their highly ordered traditional culture. However, once the break is made, social constraints apparently operational when the gang members are in the presence of community elders and family members become irrelevant, especially when rival gang members encounter one another in a conflict situation (Kodluboy, 1997).

NATIVE AMERICAN GANGS

A comparatively new phenomenon is the development of traditional street gangs among Native American youth dwelling both in cities and on reservations. The recent experience of these youth somewhat parallels the experience of youth of Southeast Asian descent, in that both groups have highly structured, traditional cultures and only recently have developed street gangs as a response to modern urban stresses. While traditional, party, and fighting gangs have been recognized in urban and rural Native American communities for two decades, only recently have these gangs taken the form, style, and functions of traditional street gangs.

In a 1996 survey of Native American youth living in the Phillips community of Minneapolis (Golden Eagles Program, 1997), 22% of 14-year-olds alleged gang affiliation. While youth gangs had been poorly represented in the Native American community prior to the summer of 1993, massive structural upheaval in the composition of gangs in Minneapolis resulted in a rapid recruitment of Native American youth into existing Chicago-style, intraethnic street gangs. As numbers grew, these Native American youth soon formed traditional, largely single-ethnic gangs. They began engaging in cafeteria-style criminal activity, including auto theft, vandalism, some drug use and sales, simple and aggravated assault, and felony firearms violations, some including gang-on-gang homicides. Several gangs adopted sacred traditional symbols, such as the medicine wheel, as gang logos.

While the development of modern-day street gangs among Native American youth in Minneapolis can be clearly followed, the parallel development of such gangs in other U.S. cities and towns requires further analysis. Once traditional street gangs develop in urban centers where there is a significant population of native youth, the common cultural practice of movement back and forth from the city to the home reservation and nearby towns becomes the mechanism for gang migration—between Minneapolis and native communities of greater Minnesota, North and South Dakota, and Wisconsin and other Central Plains states. Such movement is often precipitated by temporary or permanent family relocations as a result of family crises such as the death of a parent, or by relocation of a gang-involved youth in an effort to find a safer, non-gang environment. Relocated young gang members may or may not continue to express their gang persona in the new setting.

Federal law enforcement officials cite studies indicating the doubling of gangs on reservations since 1994 and an increase in gang-related violent crime. The Navajo Nation reports 55 gangs with 900 members, and the Salt River Pima–Maricopa Indian community near Phoenix notes the presence of 19 gangs. Gang and drug activity appears to be increasing on reservations ranging from Washington State through the Dakotas, Minnesota, and Wisconsin, as well as south to Arizona, Oklahoma, and New Mexico (von Sternberg, 1997). The Gila River Indian Community in Arizona has experienced the development of 20 gangs, primarily juvenile, with gang-related criminal activity including car theft, assault, and murder (Revere, 1997).

These gangs, with their rapid spread to rural areas and reservations, are of grave concern to Native American communities across the nation. New on the scene is the development of formal linkages with criminal adult leadership. Increasingly, linkages also are appearing with Spanish-speaking gangs at both the youth gang member and the adult levels.

Clearly, the spread of gangs to the Native American community is the result of several variables. The marginalization of native youth continues across this nation. Racism and discrimination impact such youth as they have done for generations. Movement between city centers and native communities has occurred for generations as well. What is different today is the presence of strong gang-developing forces within the cities where such youth live, as evidenced by the Minneapolis experience. What is also new is the bombardment of Native American youth with gangster music, articles about gangs, gangsters on television programs and especially in the movies, and the portrayal as role models of former or current gang members who are athletes, singers, or rappers. These images are as irresistible to some Native American youth as they are to any others.

SUMMARY

The rise and spread of youth gangs to almost every state in the union presents a major challenge to schools and the communities they serve. As communities segregate and isolate along ethnic, language, cultural, and economic lines, the opportunity for enrichment and the risk of disenfranchisement for a portion of youth will coexist. Immigration has brought a rich diversity and, simultaneously, the risk of isolating already marginalized youth. What remains hopeful and common across each generation and wave of immigration is access to public education. It is within the school—with the extension of the school into the community and the invitation of community members into the school—that the opportunity for reaching and educating these at-risk youth presents itself. Efforts at this level have the potential to reduce these youths' interest in and need for gang affiliation.

CHAPTER FIVE

Gang Violence

Aggressive acts perpetrated by youth gang members in and near secondary and primary schools appear to have grown in number in recent years, and schools increasingly have lost their "neutral turf" status. However, the disposition to injure another student intentionally—with words, fists, or bullets—rarely originates in the school. To understand youth gang aggression in the school setting, we first must look elsewhere: to the nonschool venues in which such behavior is so thoroughly taught.

AGGRESSION IN SOCIETY

Both collective and individual aggression have long been prominent and recurring features in our country. In both small and large groups, our citizens have carried forth revolution, civil war, vigilantism, feuds, agrarian and labor strife, racially motivated lynchings, student riots, and, in recent years, ever more frequent youth gang violence. At the individual level, violence has become especially acute for young people on both city and suburban streets. Between 1988 and 1992, all categories of violent crime increased substantially for youths under age 18: murder and nonnegligent manslaughter (55%), forcible rape (27%), and aggravated assault (80%). Overall, violent crime increased 29.1% (U.S. Office of Juvenile Justice and Delinquency Prevention, 1994).

Anecdotal evidence strongly suggests that this increase in youth violence is occurring for both males and females ("Youth Violence,"

1991). Teenagers in the United States are at minimum four times as likely to be murdered as are their counterparts in 21 other industrialized countries (Center to Prevent Handgun Violence, 1990).

Physical aggression is not uncommon in the home. A nationwide survey conducted in 1968 for the National Commission on the Causes and Prevention of Violence (Mulvihill, Tumin, & Curtis, 1969) revealed that 93% of survey respondents reported having been spanked in childhood, 55% had been slapped or kicked, 31% punched or beaten, 14% threatened or cut with a knife, and 12% threatened with a gun or shot at. Matters have not changed. In 1994, Straus reported that 90% of children in the U.S. received corporal punishment. Fifty-six percent had been slapped, 31% pushed or shoved, and 10% hit with an object. Between 4 and 14% of our children are physically abused (burned, bones broken, shaken severely, etc.). A survey conducted by Knox (1991) of over 1,000 members of 225 gangs revealed that 42% of the youths had been physically assaulted by a family member.

In addition to its streets and homes, the third major setting in the U.S. for the teaching and learning of aggressive behavior is the mass media: music, comics, radio, movies, and, especially, television. The heavy diet of violence offered by television in particular appears to contribute substantially to both the acquisition of aggressive behavior and the instigation of its enactment. Prime-time television in the U.S. during 1994 showed an average of six acts of violence per hour. Saturday morning cartoons portrayed 25 violent acts per hour. By age 16, the average adolescent, who views approximately 35 hours of television per week, will have seen 200,000 acts of violence, 33,000 of which are murders or attempted murders (National Coalition on Television Violence, 1994). A substantial minority of viewers have been shown to engage in copycat violence.

The pernicious effects of television violence go further, extending among the viewing audience to an increase in fearfulness, mistrust, and self-protectiveness and to a substantial decrease in sensitivity, concern, and revulsion toward violence. Higher and higher levels of violence become more and more tolerable. These and other aggression-enhancing and aggression-desensitizing effects of television have been documented in many sources (Comstock, 1983; Huesmann & Miller, 1994; Liebert, Neale, & Davidson, 1973).

Clearly, the forms of aggression so evident in our streets, homes, and mass media provide context for the individual and collective learning and expression of aggression in the schools. These forms are, as a group, "background context." But what about the immediate setting, the school itself? For most of this country's almost 50 million schoolchildren, the school day unfolds with no threats to safety and security—no fights, no weapons, no bullying, no theft. The role of school violence as an immediate context for gang aggression must therefore be kept in perspective. Yet school violence is indeed a real and growing concern.

The level of assault on teachers in U.S. public schools is sufficiently high that the vocabulary of aggression has been expanded to include what Block (1977) has called the "battered teacher syndrome": a combination of stress reactions including anxiety, depression, disturbed sleep, headaches, elevated blood pressure, and eating disorders. The National Center for Education Statistics revealed in 1992 that nearly one out of five U.S. school teachers reported being verbally abused by students, 8% reported being physically threatened, and 2% indicated they had been attacked by students during the previous year. A 1994 Metropolitan Life Insurance Company survey indicated that 11% of teachers reported being assaulted at school—in 95% of the instances by students. Eleven percent of the 2.56 million teachers in the U.S. is 270,000 people!

The seriousness of these attacks notwithstanding, it must be remembered that most aggression in U.S. schools is directed toward other students. Much of it is low-level aggression (i.e., cursing, bullying, harassment). Yet aggression has been shown to be primarily learned behavior. When low levels of its expression are both rewarded (e.g., with peer and teacher attention) and unpunished (as school personnel attend more and more exclusively to assaults, fights, and other high-level expressions), students increasingly learn "I can keep doing this" and "I can even escalate as I wish."

During the first half of 1990, approximately 9% of all students ages 12 to 19 were crime victims in the U.S.—2% the victims of violent crimes, 7% of property crimes (U.S. Department of Justice, 1991). Siegel and Senna (1991) add that "although teenagers spend only 25 percent of their time in school, 40 percent of the robberies and 36 percent of the physical attacks involving this age group occur in school" (p. 99).

A 1990 report, aptly titled *Caught in the Crossfire* (Center to Prevent Handgun Violence, 1990), fully captures the central role of firearms in the more recent surge of school violence. From 1986 to 1990, 71 people (65 students and 6 employees) were killed by guns in U.S. schools. Another 201 were seriously wounded, and 242 were held hostage at gunpoint. The American School Health Association (1989) estimates that 7% of boys and 2% of girls carry a knife to school every day.

All behaviors, certainly including aggression, are person-environment events. They are inherently interactions—that is, they result from the dual influence of the context (i.e., the environment, in the present instance including larger society, the family, the mass media, and the school setting itself) and the qualities or dispositions of the individual. While there are perhaps no "typical" gang youth, the gang literature is replete with descriptions of such youngsters that highlight their proclivity to employ violence as a way of life. They have been pictured as defiant individuals (Jankowski, 1991); impulsive (Klein, 1995); quick to misinterpret ambiguous events (a look or a bump) as a challenge or threat (Dodge, 1993); honor defending, macho, and prone to seeking "character-contests" (Sanders, 1994); reckless, irresponsible, and callous (Magdid & McKelvey, 1987); and lacking in empathy (Hare, 1970) and guilt (Gough, 1948). Knox's (1991) survey of 1,000 gang members buttresses these impressions. Forty-six percent of the youths interviewed reported experiencing serious anger control problems *daily!* Thirty-four percent had assaulted a teacher the year of the survey, 68% claimed to have shot at someone, and 39% had been physically assaultive to a family member. They averaged 10 serious fights with other youths that year.

In the decade of the 1980s, according to data provided by Sanders (1994), gang member assaults, shootings, and homicides each increased substantially. Compared to nongang delinquents, gang youth commit more—and more serious—offenses, escalate their violence more quickly, and continue their violence to a later age (Hoffman, 1996). Forty percent of all homicides in Los Angeles, Minneapolis, and Chicago were gang related, the large majority of the victims being gang members. For many of these gang youths, violence in their lives is clearly pervasive.

With violence instruction filling their lives and a predisposition to use aggression often prominent in their personalities, it is not surprising that youth gang members bring violence to school. At times violence begins with a dispute originating in the neighborhood over some real or imagined slight, drug sale, or violation of territory. The dispute then moves to or near the school. In fact, the violence may be "saved" for school, where it is anticipated that an audience will be present and that school personnel will be ready to intervene. Other times, instigation to aggression may be the mere presence of rival gang members, a bad look in the school hallway ("mad dogging," "stare-down," "thousand-yard stare"), a bump in passing, a boundary dispute, a rumor, ethnic tension, a perceived insult, a dispute over females (or males), or another event occurring within the school.

FORMS OF GANG VIOLENCE

Why it begins and whether it occurs within the school, school environs, or neighborhood, youth gang violence takes the several forms next described. In the vast majority of instances, aggression within a gang—that is, toward members of one's own gang—is verbal: criticism, cursing, ribbing, put-downs, insults. Physical violence within a gang is much less common and usually takes place as part of initiation into membership, for failure to follow important gang rules (e.g., regarding drug selling or use, or sex with a fellow member's relative), or for trying to resign from the gang at a time the gang deems premature.

Physical attacks on members of a rival gang, strangers, or fellow students or school staff are in contrast rather more frequent and can take several forms. When the fictional Jets and Sharks of *West Side Story* met in the school yard to fight it out with fists, sticks, and similar nonlethal weapons, the gang rumble became a fixed piece of American mythology. In reality, the rumble is far from a common event. Although such fights between rival gangs did take place, as often as not some last-minute, face-saving event prevented them: a flat tire, an anonymous call to police, a mix-up about the correct location for the fight. *West Side Story* is excellent theater but a poor metaphor for current gang realities.

Also largely gone from the current gang scene is the "fair fight," in which a member representing each gang, usually the leader or his "warlord," fight it out with their fists until one surrenders. Fights between gang members do occur, of course, but it is more common for one or more members of a gang to jump a rival gang member to perpetrate an assault.

In another form of aggression against a rival gang, a clique or subgroup of a gang conduct a "foray." This is an automobile excursion into a rival gang's neighborhood to flash weaponry, in order to intimidate (the show-by), or to use weaponry, in order to injure or kill (the drive-by).

Sometimes innocent citizens going about their business are the direct targets of gang violence, not just those caught by chance in the crossfire of a drive-by shooting. In what has been called "wilding," a large number of gang members maraud down an avenue, break windows, assault elderly citizens, steal purses, and generally create mayhem. The infamous case of the Central Park jogger—a young woman attacked, raped, and beaten senseless by a gang in New York City—is an example of wilding.

"Swarming" is another form of gang violence toward uninvolved citizens. One form, home invasion, began in Toronto and most commonly affected Vietnamese Canadians and Vietnamese nationals, a population believed by custom to be distrustful of banks and the police, preferring to keep their savings in their homes. There is a knock on the door at night, and when the homeowner answers, a dozen or more gang members swarm in to intimidate, steal, and injure. Swarming also refers to a half-dozen or more gang members surrounding a victim on the street, to mug or simply assault that person.

In Taiwan, where motor scooters are popular, yet another form of gang violence, "slashing," has taken place. A group of juveniles cruise past pedestrians on their scooters on a city street. With no provocation, one reaches out as he drives by and slashes at a pedestrian with a knife. Such random violence has recently been reported in the U.S., as has "bashing," in which one of a group of gang members in a cruising automobile leans out the window, baseball bat in hand, and smashes the bat against the head of a passing citizen.

A great deal of the gang violence that occurs is, in a broad sense, territorial. Traditionally, most such turf disputes concern dominion over neighborhood areas. But turf of many types can be contested: streets, parks, shopping malls, skating rinks, criminal enterprise, girlfriends, school yard and school cafeteria locations, and more. Furthermore, ownership ("This park is ours, stay out!") is but one form of turf rights. Occupancy rights ("On Sunday afternoon this park is ours, stay out!") and enterprise monopoly rights—usually claims to exclusive rights to commit certain kinds of crime, such as drug sales—are two other types. It is important to reiterate that most gang violence is not drug related. While in some cities the relation-ship between gangs and drugs is increasingly common, in most in-stances gang violence concerns the more personal matters of status, space, or perception.

SUMMARY

Aggression in youth gangs in the U.S. most appropriately should be appraised in the context of aggression in this country in general. Endemic violence provides both context and impetus for violence in our schools and by the gang members in them. In the present chapter we have outlined the nature and sources of gang violence, described its diversity of expression, and suggested its serious impact on society at large.

Part 2
Effective Interventions

CHAPTER SIX

Desirable Program Characteristics

Once a school district determines that school-age youth gangs are indeed a problem, members of the school community must consider gang intervention, prevention, and suppression programs. If the problems have developed slowly and uniformly across school and community settings, and if no crisis has yet occurred, planning can be timely and thoughtful. Potential strategies can be carefully researched, vendors scrutinized, curriculum materials reviewed, and an evaluation plan put in place before actual implementation. Fortunate is the district that follows such a course. Far more common is the circumstance that gang crime, especially gang violence, has stricken the community, inciting fear among residents and students.

Inevitably, gang problems do arise in the schools, and, rather than deal with them as gang related, administrators tend to deal with them as matters of simple discipline (Stephens, 1997). Doing so fails to recognize the unique nature of gang-related problems, however, and does little to support families and community in responding to gang activity. A discipline policy alone is no more effective in addressing the gang problem than is police suppression alone. What is needed is a comprehensive strategy involving all stakeholders.

BEST PRACTICE

The recommended strategy is to follow a best-practice model. This model assumes a data-driven system of responses and careful evaluation of outcomes. Best practice means a critical and comprehensive review of available outcome data gathered on past programs or those currently in place elsewhere. It also means the design and implementation of variations of established programs to meet the unique needs of one's own district. These systematic replications may borrow from effective or promising programs, with careful attention to important outcome measurement questions.

A less desirable alternative is for district officials, following some crisis, to make a less carefully considered selection. Often, following such a crisis—perhaps the death or wounding of a student on or near a school campus—previously unknown gang "experts" appear and offer their services, sometimes even demanding access to the students and school campus. Offers to mediate gang disputes, give motivational speeches to gang-eligible students, and develop community-based gang intervention programs are common. Frequently, the only qualification of such persons is a personal history of prior gang involvement. Rhetoric inflames a sense of urgency, and the pressure to "do something" sometimes drives administrators to make hasty decisions. School officials would be wise to move slowly before accepting any such offers.

The best-practice approach suggests that, irrespective of the incident or history underlying the move for gang prevention, intervention, and suppression programming, planning should occur in a deliberate manner. Kodluboy and Evenrud (1993) make the following suggestions:

> Any gang-focused program to be implemented within the public schools or in a collaboration between public schools and community agencies should:

1. Be related to and share the common mission and objectives of the school and school district.

2. Be public and accountable.

3. Be based on established standards of the profession or social service agency involved.

4. Have specific, written projected outcomes.

5. Have reasonable time lines for attaining the projected outcomes and meeting commitments.

6. Monitor progress toward individual and agency objectives, using simple, direct measures.

7. Be subject to external review.

8. Demonstrate social validity through broad-based community involvement of all interested parties, such as businesses, neighborhood representatives, and others.

9. Be free of cultural bias and consistent with prevailing prosocial community goals and norms. (p. 268)

In the absence of best-practice criteria, the basis for accepting or rejecting program or individual involvement will be unclear, perhaps leaving the district open to charges of favoritism, discrimination, or incompetence. A best-practice approach is defensible in that it is referenced to the professional literature, reflects common ethical and professional standards, is highly accountable and public, and allows equitable access to all potential providers and partners in the effort to keep the school safe.

Accountability and Credentials

While collaboration with social service and educational agencies is an important goal for most school districts, programs offered by such agencies range widely along a continuum of quality, competence, legitimacy, accountability, and relatedness to the mission of the public schools. Administrators must be highly selective about who is allowed access to students during the school day, or after school if the program is offered to students through official school channels. Fortunately, only rarely do persons with malicious or criminal intent attempt to gain access to students. More commonly, persons with poorly designed, or merely irrelevant, programs are those who must be avoided. These persons may have the best of intentions but may represent very poor student programming.

Kodluboy and Evenrud (1993) have suggested that for persons to work in the public school setting, they must present credentials supporting their participation in the specific activity they propose. Persons who propose to do counseling must present documentation that they are qualified by formal training and certification to do counseling. Chemical dependency workers are licensed or certified in most states and can provide such credentials. Teachers, psychologists, social workers, and counselors are all licensed and credentialed. In some intervention models, police officers offer gang resistance training or "leaving the gang" programs; they are also licensed and can provide certification of training. Therefore, it imposes no special burden to these and any other persons who offer services, whether group or individual, to provide the school with documentation.

Just because a person is a former gang member or grew up in a gang-impacted neighborhood does not mean that person is qualified to provide gang counseling. There is an increasing trend among some in this nation to view gangs as a legitimate social structure for neighborhood reorganization. This has sometimes resulted in current and former gang members offering to calm gang tensions in schools and to work with gang members. On occasion, they may suggest that their gang has evolved into a pro-youth organization. For example, the Gangster Disciples now commonly state that "GD" stands for "growth and development," thus putting a positive spin on the otherwise negative character of the gang. Rarely do such persons offer to help get gang-involved students out of gangs. Rather, they offer to "stop the violence" or to transform violent youth into prosocial youth. School officials must be wary of implementing gang values transformation programs offered by former gang members. To do so is likely to increase gang cohesion and legitimacy and is unlikely to result in reduction in gang-related problems, except in the short term.

The New York Experience

Numerous districts have encountered problems when utilizing former or current gang members in counseling or security positions. A recent example is a cautionary tale for administrators. In the fall of the 1997–1998 school year, the New York City schools investigative staff published a report regarding the Latin Kings (Flamm, Keith, & Kleppel, 1997). A school security officer, a ranking member of the Latin Kings, allegedly continued to honor his sworn role to protect students who were Latin Kings and to recruit new members into the gang. On one occasion, this security officer used his school safety officer credentials to dissuade a New York City police officer from investigating a youth gathering in a local park, telling the police officer that the gathering was a school event. In reality, the event was a gang beating of a member who had violated gang rules. In the investigative report, the authors cite numerous other incidents in which the school grounds or immediate neighborhood was used for meetings and gang business of the Latin Kings and other gangs. Among their investigative staff's recommendations was "No member of the Latin Kings, or any other similar criminal street gang, should be employed as a School Safety Officer. There is an irreconcilable conflict of interest, as the Latin Kings' own rules state that the members' duty to the gang comes ahead of any other authority" (p. 59). Persons developing gang intervention plans should give serious consideration to the New York experience.

To sum up, hiring current gang members in a security or counseling role is unwise at best and may generate more serious problems than it resolves, as evidenced by the New York experience. Even when former gang members are hired, school officials must be certain of their distance from the gang and watchful for incidents of apparent allegiance to or legitimization of the gang. They must also be certain that any such applicants have well-documented, supervised training, education, and certification, consistent with the roles for which they apply.

Factors in Hiring and Termination

While opinions differ as to whether or not one should hire former and even current gang members for security, counseling, or conflict mediation positions, one thing is certain: It is imperative for any district developing hiring criteria to assure that applicants have due process and that formal mechanisms are in place for applicants or employees to appeal rejection for or termination from employment. Such actions must be consistent with current statutes, case law, and district policies. Decisions must be based not simply on association, but on the following criteria:

1. Behavior histories (e.g., the applicant's or employee's history of violent or other criminal gang-related behavior, relevant to student interaction and inconsistent with written school district policies)

2. Behavioral commitments (e.g., stated allegiance to the gang in the form of a vow, initiation ceremony, written constitution, or written behavior guidelines for gang members, inconsistent with the written mission and policies of the school district)

3. Admitted or proven current interactions with active gang members in school or the community during the commission of delinquent or criminal gang-related activities

4. Admitted or proven current displays of gang-related behavior, such as use of gang hand signs, gang handshakes, or specific gang terms when communicating with students; displays of specific gang representations (e.g., jewelry, clothing); and/or recruitment of students to the gang

5. Expressions of gang legitimacy, such as suggesting that the gang is a prosocial organization rather than a criminal or delinquent association, to a degree inconsistent with school district mission statements or policies

6. Admitted or proven application of differential discipline or differential preference toward student members of the applicant's or employee's gang or rival gang

Consistent with the New York schools' proposed policies, these factors should be considered when developing and implementing policies regarding employees' past or present gang involvement. As always, the school district's loss-management staff and attorneys must approve all such policies and procedures.

The Gang as a Unit

While it may sometimes be necessary for school officials to deal with the gang as a group, it is never a first choice. Students generally join the gang as individuals and leave as individuals. It is preferable to intervene individually to help gang-involved students leave the gang. When school officials do find themselves dealing with a gang structure resistant to individual intervention, it is wise to use interventions demonstrated effective in altering youth commitment to gang affiliation, such as Aggression Replacement Training (Goldstein, Glick, & Gibbs, 1998), to refocus the activities of the gang, while concurrent efforts to motivate individual withdrawal from the gang proceed. Legitimizing the gang as a unit in the eyes of gang members and non-gang-involved students must be carefully avoided in the school setting. It is important to avoid using student gang leaders as go-betweens between factions or to represent their gang members in disputes. If it is absolutely essential to do so, then it is equally essential to make efforts to decrease any increased gang cohesion that might occur as a result.

The risk of increasing gang cohesion by hiring and paying former and current gang members to occupy security, counseling, or mediator positions is very real. Both gang-involved and non-gang-involved students often state that the message they receive from such hirings is that the gang is so powerful or so foreign to teachers and administrators that it is necessary to hire former or current gang members to control or even speak with students who are gang affiliated. We diminish the role of conventional adults in the lives of students when we suggest that only gang members can understand other gang members.

Should the school administration desire or be pressured to invite gang speakers or to collaborate with a community agency that employs former gang members, they should consider the provisions recommended by Kodluboy and Evenrud (1993):

1. Verify [the individuals'] status as former, rather than active, current gang members.

2. Determine that they have the educational, professional or paraprofessional skills to interact with students in a manner acceptable to school personnel.

3. Require some direct supervision or monitoring by school district employees.

4. Consult parents of both directly and indirectly involved students who will be exposed to these individuals.

5. Monitor the direct and indirect short-term and long-term effects of these individuals' activities on student behavior and school climate.

6. Determine the impact on school relationships with other agencies such as law enforcement, parole, probation and corrections.

7. Monitor the behavior of involved students in the community over time. (p. 289)

The ideal persons to work with gang members are individuals who have not been gang members but who are highly informed on gang issues.

Put It in Writing

Hiring procedures, school safety plans, outcomes, and the like are often cited but infrequently written. When written, such documents are rarely updated. When updated, such documents are often not disseminated among stakeholders. It is imperative that all mission statements, policies, plans, procedures, and outcomes be written and reviewed at least once yearly and that they be disseminated among a representative group of staff, students, parents, and community members. Such a process allows for meaningful input and engenders confidence and participant support for the system. While systems that depend upon the particular attributes and strengths of individual staff members can be highly effective in the short run, the loss of a particular individual can leave those remaining in a vulnerable position. Emphasis on written procedures allows for continuity should any key participant leave the system.

ANTECEDENT INTERVENTION

Before any intervention, especially a behavioral intervention, can be considered, it is necessary to review the basic academic strategies employed in the school. Students are unlikely to engage in prosocial behavior if they are academically disengaged. Each school must use a range of academic interventions, both group and individual, so all students may gain. This means that, irrespective of the educational or programmatic philosophy of the school, the staff will make whatever adaptations are necessary for students, especially marginal students, to learn. If students do not make reasonable academic growth, gang prevention and intervention efforts will be inefficient at best and, for high-risk individuals, completely ineffective. Simply put, if students do not derive personal reward, self-esteem, or public praise for academic success, they will seek to meet such basic adolescent needs where they are more easily acquired. Increasingly, the gang is a place to receive such experiences.

Kodluboy and Evenrud (1993) describe a behavioral systems model as it might be employed in an effective school:

1. All primary systems must first focus on immediate improvement in academic performance for all at-risk or gang-involved students. In the absence of academic progress commensurate with grade expectations, other programs are unlikely to be maximally effective and will at best lack an essential component of social validity.

2. Individual behavior management systems must focus on active teaching of positive social behaviors, include plans for promoting generalization across school settings and include maintenance components for long-term persistence of newly acquired social skills.

3. Behavior reduction strategies are necessary but only when used concurrently with written, positive prosocial skills teaching programs. Behavior reduction systems do not supplant but rather supplement positive programs.

4. Depending on the age of the student(s) directly concerned, an appropriate degree of active student involvement in program planning and monitoring should be encouraged. An informed, involved student is more likely to be a compliant and satisfied participant. Involve the student whenever possible.

5. Behavior management programs must specify both short-term and long-term outcomes, referenced to the mission, goals and objectives of the school and the community at large.

6. Behavior management programs are best implemented in the environment where the behavior is expected to occur naturally. Implementing programs directly in all school settings decreases the need for programming aimed specifically at generalization of behavior to the school setting.

7. Progress monitoring of target behaviors should use brief, direct, simple measures. The use of time-series data, taken weekly, for example, is recommended. For a student who habitually missed or came late to all classes because he was associating with gang-related peers elsewhere in the building, formative evaluation might entail weekly charting of the number of classes attended on time. Staff might ask a

formerly gang-affiliated student to self-report the number of social events attended in the company of gang-involved peers versus those where gang-involved peers were absent or in the minority. Building-wide measures might include such weekly items as the number of new graffiti reported, the number of students observed "representing" by wearing gang colors, the amount of student time devoted to extracurricular school activities or jobs, or the number of aggressive encounters where gang affiliation was a factor. Formative evaluation is preferred to summative evaluation alone.

8. Focusing on indirect measures not corroborated by direct observation of social behavior in naturalistic settings is discouraged. For example, verbal behavior of students involved in a values transformation group may not be accompanied by any observable, appropriate social behavior in school or in the community. [Measurement of gang members' behaviors should be] more influenced by what they do than by what they say (Spergel, 1990). Hagedorn's (1988) observation that gang members are highly facile in lying to social service agency representatives is advisory.

9. Parental collaboration and parent training programs are essential to both enhancing academic success and improving social competencies. A strong parent outreach component with specific activities to improve parents' skills in positive discipline and supervision, and to encourage involvement in their children's lives, is recommended. (pp. 280–281)

What is important in the preceding description of an effective school is that there is a clear definition of both precursor and outcome variables, with an emphasis on frequent direct measurement with concurrent validation. This means that any good program or program component will clearly describe the behavior of concern in plain language and in terms that can be directly observed, and will measure the outcome behavior on a frequent basis.

PROMISING PROGRAM MODELS

Each month, teachers, psychologists, social workers, counselors, and administrators find their mailboxes stuffed with mailings offering the latest and best in programs, films, and books. Frequently, the best-looking, best-marketed, or most familiar material is selected for review and implementation. Rarely do we as educators look at a new solicitation and say, "I wonder if they have any data?" Yet only by asking such questions can we select or modify programs likely to be valuable and cost-effective.

Office of Justice Programs Report

The Office of Justice Programs (OJP) has recently released a careful meta-analysis of drug, crime, and delinquency prevention programs currently in place: Specific programs are described, as are categories of programs. The outcome measures are direct and specified in terms of effect sizes and percent change in outcome measures. Each program is also rated in terms of scientific rigor; these ratings allow the reader to determine how likely the observed outcome is to be repeated if the program is implemented and analyzed. For example, a scientific rigor measure of 1 is poor, and therefore caution is advised in relying on the outcome results, whereas a rigor of 5 is likely to be quite reliable. The discussion immediately following is a summary of the OJP report, *Preventing Crime: What Works, What Doesn't, What's Promising* (Sherman, Gottfredson, MacKenzie, Eck, Reuter, & Bushway, 1997). First described are outcome studies by category: capacity building, instructional programs, redefining the group, curriculum as intervention, and law-related education. The section closes with a look at the instructional variables affecting program success.

Capacity Building

In preventing crime and delinquency, programs that build school capacity are effective. Effective programs clarify staff role and responsibilities, emphasize teaming across a wide range of participants from within the school community, establish clear goals, and implement high measurement standards. Increasing communication and cooperation among all members of the school community and using a prescriptive problem-solving model is encouraged. Such programs appear to result in significant reduction of delinquent behavior, drug use, and suspensions for misbehavior in treatment schools, as compared with control schools.

Setting clear norms for behavior and establishing specific rules include clear expression of behavioral expectations and the consistent, predictable, and fair application of discipline to all students. Such programs also emphasize classroom organization and consistent classroom management. Teachers are well trained in such practices and engage in frequent home communication regarding both good behavior and problem behavior.

Such schools also use schoolwide poster campaigns with an antiviolence theme, for example. The use of planned positive reinforcement of appropriate student behavior is integral. The balance of clear definitions of acceptable and unacceptable behavior, the concurrent use of programmed positive reinforcement for expected behavior, and consistent, specific administration of behavior reduction strategies for problem behaviors facilitates "behavioral contrast," which provides a combined overall effect greater than the use of any strategy alone. Treatment schools show reductions in drug and alcohol use as well as delinquency over time. Such programs include Program Development Evaluation, the Effective Schools Project, and a project by Kennedy and Watson (cited in Sherman et al., 1997).

Instructional Programs

Comprehensive instructional programs that stress the social competencies of problem solving, prosocial communication, social decision making, and self-control are effective to the extent that intensity, longevity, and rehearsal are involved. This means that the degree of success depends on how rigorously students are taught specific social skills, how much support they receive for practicing these skills across school environments, and how long the program lasts.

Redefining the Group

Programs that regroup high-risk students within a school—often called schools-within-schools or self-contained programs—are effective to the degree that they employ effective academic and social instruction along with strong classroom management. Alternative schools are another way of regrouping students, often removing them from the main school. While testimonials abound in support of alternative schools, few studies have been completed on such schools and even fewer have sufficient scientific rigor to guide the consumer. Because these programs serve an important safety-valve function, little motivation exists to ask important questions about their effectiveness. The meta-analysis of alternative schools conducted by Cox, Davidson, and Bynum (1995) demonstrates only "a small positive effect on school performance, school attitude and self-esteem" (p. 229). Alternative schools may be recommended on the basis of the degree of rigor they provide in terms of student selection, program intensity, clarity of objectives and methods, and degree of accountability.

Curriculum as Intervention

Curriculum-based instructional programs include such programs as DARE, GREAT, Life Skills Training, ALERT, and others. Competent studies of some drug abuse prevention and resistance programs increasingly show little effect in reducing drug use over time. Programs that emphasize basic information, fear arousal, moral appeal, and self-esteem building tend to have little, if any, effect on drug use. Programs that may include the above-mentioned features but that also emphasize specific resistance skills acquisition and rehearsal of specific refusal skills (e.g., Life Skills Training), tend to show positive effects in reducing drug use. Effective programs tend to run for an extended period of time (i.e., 6 months or more), include many rehearsal skill sessions, and program for generalization to settings other than the training setting.

The best-known specific gang resistance program is GREAT, or Gang Resistance Education and Training. This new program, in the early stages of evaluation, is viewed by some authors as promising, while others hold a less optimistic view (Sherman et al., 1997). The program offers 9 weeks of instruction by law enforcement officers, emphasizing basic information about gangs and community, conflict resolution, alternatives to gang involvement, and social responsibility. The short duration of the program, the lack of specific social skills instruction, and the lack of generalization training weaken program intensity and gang-resistance practice opportunities for students. Although the recent formative evaluation has a somewhat low score on scientific rigor, some weak but positive effects significantly favor treatment compared to control students. Because GREAT is in the early stages of implementation, its developers presumably will be responsive to making changes and additions suggested by the evaluation in progress. The need for gang resistance training demands program flexibility, and we remain optimistic that demonstrably effective gang resistance programs will arise from current initial efforts.

Law-related Education

Other instructional programs developed by federal agencies include law-related education, which emphasizes basic classroom instruction on law, citizenship, moral reasoning, ethics, and responsibility. The Office of Justice Programs review (Sherman et al., 1997) suggests law-related education programs are effective in reducing delinquency only when accompanied by high-quality classroom instruction and classroom organization, and in the context of a small student unit, such as a school-within-a-school.

Instructional Variables

It is probable that no information-based strategy alone will be effective in the absence of other social instruction and organizational variables. Those variables that make instruction effective are extensive "reliance on cognitive-behavioral training methods, such as feedback, reinforcement and behavioral rehearsal . . . rather than traditional lecture and discussion" (Sherman et al., 1997, p. 5/42).

The most promising programs for reducing delinquent behavior incorporate these instructional variables with behavioral interventions. Lochman's anger coping intervention (Lochman, 1992; Lochman, Burch, Curry, & Lampron, 1984), which utilizes extensive cognitive behavior management techniques of modifying self-talk, problem identification, other-perspective taking, learning self-inhibitory statements, and the like, showed strong effects in reducing school-based aggressive behavior. While a 3-year follow-up of aggression in the community showed only a 5% reduction, such effects were judged promising due to the high rate of offending common to the age cohort of the treatment group.

Rotheram's (1982) efforts in reducing aggressive behavior in an elementary school employed social skills training. A think-act-or-feel assertive strategy underlined the 12-week training sessions. Extensive behavioral rehearsal of desired outcome behaviors took place, as did response-specific feedback. A 1-year follow-up showed alctfd

strong, positive treatment effects, with improved academic behavior, improved social behavior, and reduced aggression.

Citing the work of Bry (1982), Sherman et al. (1997) also note that behavior modification alone has strong effects in reducing delinquent behavior. Students randomly assigned to treatment and control groups were subjected to a behavior modification program utilizing behavior-contingent points for classroom attendance, preparation, and performance, as well as for overall prosocial school behavior. Frequent parent contacts were also employed in this program. At 1-year follow-up, treatment students had significantly fewer problems at school, less substance abuse, and 15% less criminal behavior. Treatment effects at 5-year follow-up showed that students who participated in the program were 66% less likely than control students to have a juvenile record.

Other Analyses of Program Effectiveness

In a draft report written for the National Youth Gang Center, Howell (1996a) also reviews promising youth gang programs and strategies. Comprehensive community-wide approaches such as that conducted by Spergel (1996) in the Little Village Gang Violence Reduction Project, appear promising and are recommended. This project involved two extremely violent gangs in a specific neighborhood of Chicago. The strategies targeted violent or potentially violent individual gang members with increased probation and police supervision, along with suppression. Concurrently, social services and job and educational opportunities were provided to the target youths. Treatment significantly reduced gang violence.

In its comprehensive strategy for serious, violent, and chronic juvenile offenders, the U.S. Office of Juvenile Justice and Delinquency Prevention (1995) provides communities with a blueprint for coordinating a true continuum of education, prevention, and intervention. The strategy incorporates a model of graduated sanctions for juveniles who fail to respond to low-level interventions. The units of this program include public education, gang resistance training, home-based family intervention, school programs such as High/Scope, individual and group services such as social skills training and job counseling, community development, community policing, input from gang members regarding needs, and active participation of community leaders. Howell (1996a) describes specific examples of this model, such as the House of Umoja in Philadelphia, Multi Systematic Therapy in Texas (which focuses on reclaiming current gang members), and the 8% Early Intervention Program of Orange County, California, which has specifically utilized the graduated sanctions component of the OJJDP model.

Perhaps the most impressive model program is the Boston Gun Project, described by Kennedy, Piehl, and Braga (1997). This project added an essential element to the comprehensive programming model of "coerced use reduction" of firearms. Essentially, community, local, state, and federal agencies formed a cooperative in informing persons at risk for gun offenses (primarily youth gang members in the Boston area), vertical prosecution, gun tracing, and true zero tolerance for violent gang behavior. Prior to the implementation of the program, the estimated gang lifetime risk (i.e., being in a gang between the ages of 16 and 24) of a gang member's succumbing to a violent death was a startling one in seven chance. Early follow-up results show a dramatic reduction in youth homicides, apparently as a function of the entire community's having "drawn a line in the sand," which all involved agencies then enforced with unparalleled consistency.

CAUTIONARY TALES

Over time, many strategies developed to address the needs of essentially typical students who are experiencing the normal bumps and bruises of life have been extended to high-risk youth, including delinquent and gang-involved youth. These techniques—including peer strategies, counseling, tutoring, mentoring, and recreational activities—are all currently in use to reduce crime and delinquency. Unfortunately, rarely do the persons or agencies recommending or utilizing such strategies look to outcome data to verify effectiveness. When school officials implement such programs, they must apply rigorous standards of accountability. Frequent, direct measurement of program effects is required, not only in terms of consumer satisfaction but also in terms of increases in academic achievement, decreases in problem behaviors, increases in attendance, and so forth. Because supportive data are weak if not absent for many of these strategies, particularly as they have been applied with gang-affiliated youth, each school becomes an experimental, clinical trial of the program's usefulness. In a time of diminishing resources, applying such rigorous standards is necessary to defend continued program funding.

Peer Strategies

One well-known strategy, peer counseling, as typified by several variations of Positive Peer Culture, has been reviewed by Gottfredson (1987). Commonly in use in corrections facilities and schools for troubled students, this strategy assumes that troubled peers are the best counselors for other troubled youth. The data, however, seem to indicate that such interventions are more harmful than helpful. High-school youths in such treatment groups display more, not less, problem behavior than control youths, more school tardiness, poorer attitudes, more problems with parents, more overall antisocial behavior, more delinquency, and more frequent association with delinquent youth. It appears that such programs may increase the problems of troubled youth through group reinforcement of anti-social attitudes and through simple increased proximity to delinquent peers (Gottfredson, 1987).

Also popular are peer mediation and peer conflict resolution. While individual schools often report excellent results with peer mediation, rarely are the treatment controls in place that would allow any real conclusions about the relevant variables. For example, if peer mediation replaces adult mediation services, the overall time a student has for mediation may actually be increased, irrespective of who is conducting the mediation. The conclusion might then be that increased time available for mediation, not the fact that peers are conducting the mediation, is the relevant variable.

Few, if any, adequately controlled studies show any positive benefit from peer mediation programs in reducing student conflicts (Sherman et al., 1997). Interestingly, Tobler's (1992) meta-analysis suggests some benefit from peer counseling when used in substance abuse programs. The reviewers caution that because of the absence of well-controlled studies of peer mediation, the jury is still out. This means that if a school chooses to use peer mediation, all would benefit from careful application of experimental strategies to program implementation. We believe that peer mediation may indeed prove useful as part of a comprehensive program of gang prevention. What is unknown is which critical elements are important and which are irrelevant.

Counseling Strategies

Counseling may be the most common intervention strategy for all youth, including gang-involved and delinquent youth. There is something logical and familiar about sitting down with troubled or troubling youths and discussing the error of their ways, dispensing some parental/professional advice along the way. Counseling, however, is generally used to help persons who are experiencing problems common to everyday living. Intervening with gang-impacted and delinquent youth rarely fits that mold—the everyday life problems of youth living in gang-ridden neighborhoods are far more extreme than anticipated by the counseling model. When Sherman et al. (1997) review single studies and meta-analyses of the effect of counseling on delinquent behavior, they cite the work of Lipsey (1992), who in reviewing 24 studies showed counseling interventions to be the least effective among interventions for reducing delinquent behavior. The effect size is essentially zero. This does not mean that counseling for problem youths should never be employed, but rather that counseling must be done in the context of other activities demonstrated to be effective, such as behavior management, cognitive behavior management, Aggression Replacement Training (Goldstein et al., 1998), and so forth.

Another popular intervention involves student support groups, such as those for children of drug-abusing parents. According to Sherman et al. (1997), half of the money from the Drug-Free Schools and Communities goes to supporting such counseling groups. Unfortunately, Sherman et al. found not a single evaluation study that justified removing students from academic or social skills instruction to participate in such groups or that justified funding for school personnel to conduct such groups. Should a school choose to conduct a student support group, formative and summative outcome measures must be designed to assess the use of student time and staff resources. Current use of such strategies across widely divergent student groups suggests little such deliberate planning.

Tutors

Sherman et al. (1997) also reviewed a well-designed program that combined academic tutoring with twice-monthly counseling to increase school attachment. A total of 869 students were randomly assigned to treatment and control groups. While treatment group members performed better than controls on academic gain measures as a function of the tutoring, there was no effect on delinquency. Interestingly, the treatment group engaged in more drug use than did the control group, probably as a function of increased treatment group contacts with other troubled youth in the counseling groups. The role of tutors, then, might be seen to be increasing basic academic performance, a known protective factor for students, rather than some ancillary purpose. It is suggested that peer-counseling groups as a part of peer-tutoring programs should be decreased, if not eliminated, and emphasis placed on the tutoring itself, perhaps with conventional peer tutors.

Mentors

A popular and highly promoted strategy reviewed by Sherman et al. (1997) is mentoring. Schools, newspapers, television, and radio tout the importance of mentoring for troubled youth. The U.S. Office of Juvenile Justice and Delinquency Prevention has itself advanced 19 million dollars for mentoring programs. As with other well-marketed if not data-based solutions common in our schools and communities, only a few controlled school-based mentoring studies were available for analysis. In summary, Sherman et al. found that the studies were methodologically weak, did not provide any data on crime or delinquency by participants, did show positive effects for school attendance, and remain an unstudied strategy for reducing delinquency or drug abuse. It should be noted that one controlled strategy of community-based mentoring found positive effects on drug abuse but did not measure criminal or delinquent behavior. Perhaps the addition of a well-designed and supervised community-based mentoring program would provide the prosocial supervision and instruction students need at the end of the school day to stay away from gangs.

Recreation and After-School Activities

The image of rescuing wayward youth from the clutches of street gangs fills the American consciousness. Indeed, many persons, including ourselves, have personally known gang-involved youth who have left the gang behind after they became involved in some well-supervised athletic activity. However, when this image drives funding of untested and unevaluated programs, problems arise. Instances have occurred of young gang members being encouraged to become a legitimate sports team, then who continued to remain gang-affiliated and delinquent primarily as a function of their continued association through the team. The simple fact that gang members behave appropriately during a leisure activity or sporting event does not mean that they discontinue their antisocial behavior when off the dance floor, court, or field. Sherman et al. (1997) note that research has not established a relationship between time spent in leisure activities and delinquency. However, it is critical to note that time spent on activities related to conventional goals and expectations, such as time spent doing homework, is related to reductions in delinquency.

Programs specifically reviewed by Sherman et al. include after-school programs, drop-in centers, weekend programs, and special activities such as dances and community service projects. The only apparent value of such activities is that they may reduce behavior problems during the time they actually occur (i.e., at times supervision would otherwise not exist). The activities themselves appear to be unrelated to delinquency prevention. Simply stated, you cannot steal a car while you are actually playing basketball, but being on a team does not prevent you from stealing a car before or after the game. Basketball is not intrinsically curative, nor should we expect it to be. Indeed, the most visible and controversial activities substitution program known to the public is "midnight basketball." The evaluators find that "Midnight basketball programs are not likely to reduce crime. The evidence from meta-analyses of drug prevention programs suggests no behavioral effect of such programs and the few studies that have examined effects on delinquency or antisocial behavior suggest no effect" (Sherman et al., 1997, p. 5/52).

Again, the only value such a program might have would be to provide supervision when it would otherwise be lacking. Even in such a situation, are the youth most at risk likely to attend such programs, and do such programs draw youth mainly from other supervised activities, such as their homes? What risks do participants run when traveling from home to another supervised site? Is basketball a preferred alternative supervised activity? We have noted from personal experience that some alternative activities, such as use of a park and recreation center gymnasium, may attract only one gang, and only one or a few ethnic groups. Indeed, it is common for a given park or recreation center to become the gathering place of one group to the exclusion of others. Attracting those who most need attracting to supervised activities during high-risk times of day remains a significant problem.

While Sherman et al. note the importance of supervision and its central role in reducing crime and delinquency, they also note that programs emphasizing supervision must be designed not only to enhance positive effects, but also to reduce the negative impact of grouping problem youth. They single out the potential of programs such as Boys and Girls Clubs of America for reducing youths' criminal behavior, probably through their broad range of alternative program activities and the community context in which they operate.

Overview of Recommendations

Among other recommendations, the OJP report concludes that, to strengthen school-based prevention and intervention efforts, the following must occur:

◁ Support multi-year prevention efforts, e.g., programs that span the elementary school years, the middle school years, and the high school years rather than single year programs.

◁ Support multi-component prevention efforts that include the environmental-change and individual strategies that have been shown to work in some settings under some conditions and whose positive results have been replicated:

Programs aimed at building school capacity to initiate and sustain innovation.

Programs aimed at clarifying and communicating norms about behaviors.

Comprehensive instructional programs that focus on a range of social competency skills (e.g., developing self-control, stress-management, responsible decision-making, social problem solving, and communication skills) and that are delivered over a long period of time to continually reinforce those skills.

Behavior modification programs and programs that teach "thinking skills" to high-risk youths. . . .

◁ Reduce funding for program categories (counseling students for delinquency prevention, alternative activities such as recreation and community service activities in the absence of more potent prevention programming for drug prevention, and instructional drug prevention programs focusing on information dissemination, fear arousal, moral appeal, and affective education) known to be ineffective. (Sherman et al., 1997, p. 5/62)

When first reading OJP review, one is tempted to despair and ask, "Does anything work?" This is especially true for dedicated and committed professionals whose personal identities are enmeshed with programs shown to be ineffective. It is imperative to review the data carefully and agree to disagree when necessary, to collect data to examine why a discredited program actually seems to be working in a specific situation, and to examine what critical variables are actually at work in an apparently effective program so that others might efficiently—without wasting time, money, or human resources—replicate only those critical aspects. The statement "I wouldn't have seen it if I hadn't believed it" is true of program planning, development, implementation, and marketing. The sheer difficulty of the task itself makes it hard enough for educators to implement effective programs. It is unnecessary to waste a single moment or a single dollar on programs that have not proven themselves or that have in fact been shown to be ineffective.

SUMMARY

The essential variables of a successful program are as follows:

◁ Prevention: Programs should include a prevention component—enhanced supervision, enhanced academic or social skills, or other development. In addition, they should include an instructional component on gang resistance, with skills rehearsals or recreation, and with enhanced supervision and instruction during times of greatest risk.

◁ Prosocial focus: Programs should focus on the development and maintenance of affective and functional conventional social skills and beliefs.

◁ Comprehensiveness: Narrow programs must be presented in a broader context to cover the needs of the target population. Piecemeal programs tend to be ineffective and frustrating for program staff and youth alike.

◁ Coordination: Effective programs interact with and cooperate with affiliated persons and agencies. After-school programs should keep open communication (with signed informed consent) with the schools they serve. Poor or no attempts to communicate result in programs that are far less effective than they otherwise might be.

◁ Youth input: Without input from youth, either in initial program development or at least during ongoing evaluation, programs will falter and fail to serve. While no program can serve all youth in a community, input from youth can allow development of selective programs for different constituencies within a single neighborhood.

◁ Prescriptiveness: Programs that assess a particular need and then program to meet and exceed that need are more likely to be effective than are programs set up with the more general hope that they will do something useful.

◁ Program integrity: Also known as "fidelity of treatment," this means that the outline of the program is observed faithfully and that the implementation is complete and comprehensive.

◁ Program intensity: This concerns the level, amount, dosage, or quantity of the program and requires that enough resources be allocated to conduct the activities that define the program. It also means that sufficient resources are allocated for enough time each session, day, week, or month, over enough weeks or months, to see an effect. The time period must of course be defined before the program is implemented.

◁ Evaluation: Direct, observable, countable, scalable measures of success must be developed and written before program implementation, with a written statement of when measurement activities will occur over the course of the program.

◁ Specific outcomes: "If you don't know where you are going, any road will take you there" is true for all evaluations of human behavior. Programs that specify ahead of time exactly what they hope to accomplish (i.e., what they will measure) are more desirable than those that employ vague indicators of success.

◁ Standards: While *novel, bold,* and *revolutionary* often describe valued human endeavor, they are highly risky values when selecting a youth-serving program. Programs that reference the standards of the community, of a profession, and conventional values and behaviors are far more desirable than those that express more radical values.

◁ Timeliness: Programs should be determinate in length, with summative evaluation in meaningful terms at the end of the defined term. Proposals that claim, "We will let you know when we get there" are best met with the response "We will let you know when you are more specific about your timelines."

◁ Monitoring of progress: Formative evaluation proposals (i.e., as the program proceeds, rather than at the end of the fiscal year) are preferable. Formative, ongoing, direct evaluations can help guide program evolution if done so in an orderly, prescriptive manner.

◁ External review: Any program reluctant to allow outside examination is suspect, as is any program claiming that members of a certain race or class cannot perform a competent evaluation. While it is appropriate to include like-race and like-class persons on review or oversight boards, evaluation remains essentially a neutral process and, while never totally removed from racial and class politics, can always be undertaken by competent race- and class-sensitive evaluators.

◁ Validity: That which uplifts and improves the conditions of the individuals and populations being served is socially valid. Basically, a program is socially valid if the answer is yes to the question "Does this really matter to the kids, families, and communities being served?"

◁ Cultural bias: Defining bias can be an endless polemic between various constituencies and consumers. It is necessary to carefully define program components, activities, measurement outcomes, and persons involved in the day-to-day activities to decrease the potential for bias. Programs that address ethnic issues openly often find strong differences of opinion as to what values are to be defined, respected, and included in program activities and measurement goals. Planned, comprehensive efforts should be made to include input by leaders, activists, neighbors, business persons, educators, parents, gang-involved and non-gang-involved students, law enforcement officials, and others. Few cultural monoliths exist, and program developers must often choose between divergent viewpoints. An inclusive process before selecting a program at the least ensures that all stakeholders and commentators have been heard.

CHAPTER SEVEN

Controlling the School Environment

Controlling the school environment might mean "If the adults don't control the school environment, then the students will do so." Another common assumption is that control refers only to suppression or punitive activities. While school personnel do indeed often find themselves using suppression and punishment, behavior reduction strategies are only a small part of effective control of the school environment. Indeed, overuse of such strategies indicates a failure of planning or inadequate use of prevention strategies.

Controlling the school actually involves prevention and intervention procedures, educational activities, physical structures, adult and student behavioral expectations, and parent and community partnerships—including law enforcement, parole and probation, and physical characteristics of the surrounding neighborhood. School control requires an active, responsive partnership among school personnel, students, their families, and the community.

The reason to control the school campus and adjacent areas is to provide a safe environment in which all students can learn and that in addition is inviting to parents and interested community members, adds to the stability and social organization of the immediate neighborhood and the greater community, and allows students to practice behaviors that upon graduation will allow them the greatest number of life choices. Documentation of the urgency of controlling the school campus is widely available (J. Burke, 1991; N.D. Burke,

1993; Donahue, 1989; Flamm et al., 1997; Goldstein, 1994; Goldstein & Conoley, 1997; Goldstein & Huff, 1993; Harrington-Lueker, 1992; Kodluboy, 1994; Koklanaris, 1994; National League of Cities, 1994; Prophet, 1990; Stephens, 1993).

As a metaphor for conceiving the essential elements that make for best practice in controlling the school environment, one might consider a popular Eastern European folk object, the hollow nesting doll. First one sees a single large doll. The two halves of the doll separate, and inside one finds another smaller doll, which conceals yet another, even smaller doll. The number of smaller dolls within the large doll depends upon the dollmaker's objectives. However many dolls there are, each is complementary to the one before and after. A similar complementary layering is central to an effective school control plan. An effective plan begins with consideration of outside control issues and includes the neighborhood(s) from which students come, the immediate neighborhood of the school, and the physical characteristics of the school campus. Concern then moves to issues within the school itself and concerning staff selection and training. Finally, the focus is on emergency responses and special policies and procedures for high-risk activities.

NEIGHBORHOOD ISSUES

Neighborhood issues can be subdivided into two main concerns, those present in the broad area from which students are drawn and those present immediately adjacent to the school campus. While some schools draw only from a single neighborhood, it is more common for schools to draw from two or more diverse neighborhoods. If even one of these neighborhoods has an evolving or critical mass of gang members, it is likely that some gang-related behavior will be present in the school. In its simplest form, a single gang may exist in a school. In such an instance, gang-involved students may display gang clothing, symbols, language, or graffiti mainly as an expression of self-identity in contrast to other distinguishable groups of students on campus, rather than as a specific gang message. Disruptive or outright criminal gang-related behavior in such situations is unlikely and generally has a low impact within the school and between students when it does occur.

However, even in such apparent low-risk situations, dangerous problems may occur. In one large, mainly white, affluent suburb of a Midwestern city, a small number of former inner-city African American youth gang members enrolled in a school, as a result of their parents' fleeing the city for a better, safer life. On two occasions within a year, rival gang members arrived at the school to challenge their former enemies with firearms. Visible, known gang members in a school, even when the school is otherwise removed from neighborhood, economic, and social risk factors, can provide the context for gang-related violence. Even in low-risk situations where there are few gang members, a comprehensive yet proportionate response is appropriate.

When two or more gangs are present in a school, even in an otherwise low-risk neighborhood, gang challenges are more likely. Commonly, rival gang members will represent their gang to seek parity with, if not greater status than, their rivals. Graffiti challenges, staring confrontations, shows of force, and attempts to control access to parts of the building or campus commonly occur. Non-gang-involved students watch school staff to see if prompt, proportional, and effective responses are forthcoming.

Another common scenario is for a school in a neighborhood of average socioeconomic status to draw from multiple areas, some of which house students who are members of rival gangs. In cities where economic and social ghetto formation is present, a sadly increasing phenomenon is the presence of one or more established street gangs in a school located in a heavily gang-impacted neighborhood. In such situations, critical issues face administrators on a daily basis. Here the most comprehensive gang prevention and intervention planning is necessary.

The Path to the Schoolhouse Door

Getting students to and from school is the first concern for school administrators. Students may arrive on foot, by public or school bus, in parents' cars, or in vehicles driven by other students. Each mode of transportation requires consideration when students traverse dangerous areas. Students waiting at bus stops, on buses passing through rival gang neighborhoods, or walking to school past areas frequented by or "claimed" by gang youth present special security and safety concerns. It is necessary for school personnel responsible for bus safety to listen carefully for and record all instances of student harassment that occur at bus stops, on the bus, or on common routes to and from school. This documentation may take the form of a simple incident checklist to be completed by school safety personnel, bus drivers, and school building staff responsible for bus loading and unloading. This form can also be used to interview parents, students, or other observers who report problems students encounter going to or from school. The resultant database can then be evaluated by authorities for patterns of gang activity that occur between students' homes and the school campus. The reason for this vigilance is that students who live in or pass through troublesome neighborhoods often are truant because they fear assault or intimidation by local gang members. Simply put, students will not come to school if they cannot do so safely. Yet school security personnel and local law enforcement cannot respond effectively to harassment if they have inadequate information. Developing a uniform database serves the needs of all interested persons.

A uniform database also provides authorities with information to address specific problems more efficiently. If, for example, a gang member who is on probation or parole engages in the gang-related threat, intimidation, or assault of a student passing to or from school, documentation of such behavior through a common interview form can be forwarded to the proper authorities (if allowable under data privacy laws) as a condition of parole or probation. The court officer supervising the gang member can then enforce that individual's conditions of community release. Likewise, school officials can use the information to develop an appropriate individualized intervention plan for a student who frequently appears in the database for gang-related behavior problems.

In brief, asking the right questions of student victims and witnesses can provide law enforcement and corrections personnel, as well as school authorities, with the information to decrease gang intimidation community wide, through consistent enforcement of local laws, enforcement of parole or probation conditions, and the development of individual student gang intervention behavior plans.

An alert bus driver who passes through troublesome gang territory may notice a significant increase or change in gang graffiti, such as increased crossing-out of rival gang graffiti, crossed-out names of students who attend a given school, or blatant threats to known students. If forwarded to school safety officials, such information can increase the school's effectiveness in preventing gang violence and allow the school to be more responsive to immediate parent and community concerns regarding safety. The safety of individual high-risk students can be better addressed if threats are discerned quickly and appropriate prevention and intervention actions taken.

An interview form might include the following information:

◁ Date, time, and location of incident/observation

◁ If perpetrators present, manner of dress, terminology used, hand signs displayed, tattoos observed, weapons indicated or shown, vehicles present or used, age and gender

◁ If graffiti, location, date noted, photo taken, significant messages, and so forth

◁ If victim, impact on victim

◁ If police report made, case number, public portion of report, and so on

◁ School district response (e.g., suspension), increased school district safety patrol of area where incident occurred, local police increased patrol of area (during target time of incident, etc.)

◁ Other information (e.g., whether parent files criminal complaint with local or school authorities, perpetrator is disciplined by school authorities, investigation is begun, etc.)

All incident forms should be put in the school's files for easy access, future reference, and appropriate follow up at the building level. Copies of the forms should then be forwarded to a central or area office for review by the proper school security coordinator. It is impossible to make appropriate decisions regarding allocation of increasingly scarce resources without adequate and timely data. Too often, critical incidents (e.g., a shooting on or near campus) drive resource allocation; by contrast, the careful and ongoing collection and analysis of basic incident data allow for rational decision making. Responses based on data analysis may prevent or reduce the frequency of future incidents and allow for more appropriate resource allocation.

The range of responses to problems in distant neighborhoods and along bus and walking routes to school is varied. Close collaboration and information exchange between school officials and community police or crime prevention staff working in other neighborhoods will be necessary and should be coordinated by the school's safety officer.

When a transient problem is discerned, it may be necessary to provide short-term escort of buses by school district and perhaps police patrol officers until the problem is resolved. When data suggest a chronic condition, an ongoing visible presence of school district, police, or community neighborhood patrols may be necessary at

problem sites. Extra police patrols may be advisable along designated "safe routes" to and from a school during the hours students
travel. If a city designates or licenses neighborhood student "safe
houses" where students can take refuge if fearful or pursued, such
houses should be placed along designated safe routes. Parents and
students always must be fully informed as to the limitations of and
reasonable expectations for a designated safe route. In this time of
increasing random violence and use of firearms by gang members
and others, safety is, sadly, always a relative term.

On the Bus

The bus ride itself can present major safety concerns for students,
both those who are gang involved and those who are not involved
but who fear becoming the victims of an intergang rivalry. Bus drivers
must have carefully updated student lists so that intruders cannot
board. It is not uncommon for rival gang members to wait for victims
at a bus stop or to board a bus to assault or intimidate bus riders
who are members of rival gangs. Drivers should have assigned seating so problem students may be separated and to prevent student
confrontations as to who may sit in which seat. Should gang graffiti
appear on the interior of the bus, seating lists can help investigators
determine who should be interviewed. Drivers must check the bus
before and after each route, not only for sleeping students, but also
for vandalism, especially gang graffiti.

Some school districts employ bus aides or monitors to control
students' problem behavior. While such a plan is often useful in
influencing students who exhibit minor behavior problems, few data
exist to suggest efficacy of aides in preventing or responding to major
incidents. Often the report of the aide is disputed by students and
their parents, especially if the consequences for the misbehavior
are significant. Also, while the bus is moving, aides cannot move
about to reinforce good behavior and intervene with problem
behavior. They also cannot see students surreptitiously apply graffiti
to bus seats. To address these problems, some districts have installed

fixed video cameras on problem routes. In many applications, on any given day the fixed camera box may or may not contain an actual camera. The benefit of such a system is that disputes among alleged perpetrators, their parents, and school officials are quickly resolved by reviewing the disinterested video.

Neighborhood Trouble Spots

The second major area of concern is the neighborhood immediately adjacent to the school campus. Issues may include nearby liquor stores, which draw alcohol-related problems; drug selling areas or drug houses; stores that sell tobacco to underage users, thus drawing gatherings of youths; single-family and multifamily housing where gun offenses have been documented; abandoned or boarded-up houses, which may shield criminal activity or other threats to students; poorly defined boundaries between school and public areas, thereby drawing undesirable persons onto campus; or traffic patterns that allow easy access and egress for trouble-inclined drivers and their passengers. Strategies to reduce risk from these sources often require close cooperation between school district and community officials.

City resources may be engaged in a cooperative effort when data are collected to prove that a nearby business, such as a liquor store, draws problem drinkers, exchange of alcohol between adults and underage drinkers, fights between problem drinkers, and so on. Because such problems present a demonstrable danger to staff and students, it is appropriate for the school district to address the issue through all available legal and civil means. Options include enhanced police patrols, physical abatement of adjacent problem parking lots, restricted business hours, or other responses, as well as closing the problem property through local nuisance laws.

Some business owners are themselves troubled when disruptive gang members frequent their businesses, refuse to leave, intimidate or demand "protection" money or merchandise, or draw violence and vandalism from rival gangs. In such instances, effective strategies include random, unannounced visits by city licensing inspectors, who look for underage alcohol or tobacco purchases; random, frequent visits by parole officers, who closely monitor their charges; increased use of the business by community members, intent on taking back their neighborhoods and neighborhood businesses; frequent stops inside the business by both patrol officers and officers assigned to community crime prevention and community policing; and teaching business owners how to dissuade problem customers and make the business more attractive to conventional customers. Such strategies have helped businesses free themselves of problem customers, who drive away conventional community members. This in turn makes the school and community more inviting.

Constructive Engagement: Community Policing of the School

While community members view small police substations as highly desirable, few data justify claims that they deter crime adjacent to the school. Gang members and others intent on controlling areas adjacent to the school are more impressed with interventions that directly affect them. A police officer who drives by a group of gang members has less impact than an officer who stops and engages gang members in a pointed conversation. Establishing gang members' identities denies them the anonymity that allows much gang crime.

During school hours, identity checks of minors, with an eye toward truancy reduction, are highly desirable. A field identity card, written by a police officer who legally stops and interviews a gang member, often provides the gang member with the motivation to leave the area. The field identity card should list the name, age, description, and present associates of the individual, as well as the nature of the activity that drew the school security or police officer's attention. Should criminal gang activity occur later in the day, the existence of a field identity card can aid investigators in arresting the perpetrator. For such interventions to occur, the school must develop a close relationship with the police department, and community crime prevention and school liaison officers should encourage and support such police contacts with gang members. While it is common for school officials and police officers initially to view each other with some suspicion, it is essential to put aside such stereotypical beliefs, identify a common ground, and increase regular and open communication while respecting data privacy regarding individual students.

The High-Risk Dismissal

Circumstances may arise in which the threat of violence between rival gang members warrants—for either their protection or that of other students in the school—special, high-risk dismissal procedures. These procedures might involve the following sequence:

1. Assign administrators and police or security officers to paired teams.

2. Assign duties and posts.

3. Disseminate information on "major players" to key staff.

4. Monitor motor vehicle access to campus.

5. Isolate major players 15 minutes before dismissal.

6. Assign administrators to escort sequestered students to buses or cars.

7. Instruct sequestered students to leave school grounds.

8. Dismiss other students by location in school and on a staggered basis, if appropriate.

9. Instruct bus students to board without delay.

10. Move buses out rapidly.

11. Maintain high visibility of administrators and officers throughout.

Controlling High-Risk Congregations

Frequently, juvenile or adult gang members convene near the school in a manner that disrupts the educational process—for example, by blocking pedestrian traffic, intimidating students (especially rival gang members), engaging in fights, or simply playing loud music. In such instances, it may be possible to persuade a court that such individuals should be prohibited from congregating near the school.

If the individuals are students, they may be discouraged from congregating with other gang members outside the school after school hours. If they are not students, and if the school or community can present evidence that the presence of these individuals represents a threat to the safety of the school, staff, or students, school district officials may request that the gang members be prevented from congregating near the school during school hours and during all school functions, such as dances or sporting events. Trespass laws may be used as appropriate following review by school district attorneys and as consistent with current state and local laws. Past incidents of gang assaults, gang fights, and increased school truancy by students who fear the gang presence may persuade the court to order that members of the troublesome gang refrain from appearing at school events. If gang members who are on parole or probation cause repeated problems as a function of their gang membership and gang-related behavior, the court may be asked to enforce or add "no gang contact" terms to the gang members' terms of release. Close collaboration between school district attorneys and the juvenile and adult parole and probation departments should be sought when specific criminal gang behavior requires remedy.

Neighborhood Infrastructure

The addresses of abandoned, boarded-up buildings or other properties that create a demonstrable hazard or are of concern to students or parents should be forwarded to the proper local authorities. A school district representative assigned to follow such issues should monitor city activities and the schedule of abatement to ensure that the swiftest possible action is taken.

Vigilance is also necessary in monitoring city and individual graffiti abatement and efforts to prevent deterioration adjacent to the school. Few things are more indicative of community decline than the presence and accumulation of gang graffiti, broken windows, and abandoned buildings. Families do not want to live in or send their children to schools in such neighborhoods. Before being removed, graffiti should be recorded (and dated) by local authorities and, if of direct significance to the school, by school officials. The process of graffiti removal should be complete within 48 hours of notification by the property owner, if the graffiti are on private property, or within 24 hours of discovery, if the graffiti are on public property. Some neighborhood beautification programs should receive concurrent public support from school officials. Indeed, some initiatives and partnerships, such as the federal and local anticrime partnership known as "Weed and Seed," often invite or require participation by local school officials. School officials and students should participate in such activities as appropriate and consistent with school district goals. Such programs represent a rare opportunity for school personnel and parents to access and influence local, state, and federal agencies directly in neighborhood improvement.

Where schools require community service, neighborhood beautification activities, community graffiti "paint-outs," flower plantings, vacant lot clean-ups, and the like, these opportunities should be considered as offerings to students to complete their course requirements. School officials must carefully consider students' safety before permitting participation in any such project. If a risk of intimidation, assault, or retribution to project participants is present or may be reasonably anticipated, such risks must be assessed, addressed (i.e., by increased police presence at the activity), and communicated to the participants and their parents. Participating in a "take back the neighborhood" march or vigil is a matter of conscience for individual families and students. However, some activities may be simply too risky for student participation, and school officials must candidly communicate such concerns to potential participants without delay, while concurrently withdrawing school endorsement.

Critical Incidents

When gunfire is exchanged between gang members near campus, safety issues quickly rise to the forefront of concern for community officials, school officials, parents, and students. Kodluboy (1997), Kodluboy and Evenrud (1993), Goldstein and Huff (1993), Prophet (1990), Stephens (1997), the National League of Cities (1994), Long (1992), and others have cited numerous instances of gunfire on and near school campuses while students are present. Even when students are not injured, nothing will more quickly destroy a sense of safety and create fear than gunfire. Immediate, visible, calm, and proportional district response is necessary.

School personnel should meet with local law enforcement officials and review all public information regarding an incident. Available crime incident data for the area adjacent to the school should also be reviewed. Detailed dot maps of the area will show index crimes, keyed to specific addresses and intersections. By reviewing such maps across the previous 12 months, school and law enforcement personnel will be able to discern whether incidents are increasing, decreasing, or moving closer to or farther away from the school campus. The school liaison officer, gang unit officer (if available), and school security officer can then determine what steps will be necessary to prevent, or at least reduce the risk of, future critical incidents.

All concerned should discuss the critical incident frankly and calmly, exploring both short- and long-term plans of action. While a dramatic response to the incident is sometimes seen by school officials as necessary to reassure students and their families, in reality, a quiet, calm, confident, and, above all, proportional response is far more likely to evoke community confidence. Minimizing, denying, or diverting attention from the exact location or severity of an event is even more destructive. For example, when school officials attempt to minimize a gang-related shooting by saying it occurred across the street from the school rather than on the school's side of the street, their credibility comes into question. The basic rule of effective communication with parents and the media is to be honest, concise, brief, confident, and accurate. If the spokesperson does not know the answer to a question, the correct response is "I do not know—I will get back to you." The obligation is then to find the answer and indeed get back to the questioner. All answers must indicate that the school is taking the matter seriously and in proportion to the severity of the problem. Both overreaction and minimizing are incorrect responses to crisis. Dishonesty with parents or the media is never justified. While it is necessary to follow all data privacy guidelines when meeting with parents or the media, it is inappropriate to hide behind such laws when it is unnecessary to do so.

Even in the midst of careful planning and discussion, because extreme incidents require an immediate response, it may be necessary to increase police presence on and around campus immediately following a shooting, for the period of time necessary to complete a careful data review. Should the review suggest further incidents are likely, it will be important to determine what preventive measures are necessary.

Because such responses, especially those as visible as uniformed police presence, may themselves generate events requiring further action by school personnel, care must be taken to respond proportionally to the documented threat and consistently with trends apparent from the data. When the data review, consultation with law enforcement authorities, and discussion with members of the school and community suggest a critical incident is indeed an isolated event, a temporary increase in police presence along with careful, low-level incident planning within the school campus boundaries may be all the response necessary. When the review leaves the situation unclear, an increased, permanent change in the school safety plan may be required (Kodluboy, 1997; Kodluboy & Evenrud, 1993). Locking previously unlocked doors, increased within-building and campus patrols, increased police patrols, and so forth may all be considered. In some instances, the data review will direct the school to dramatically modify its school safety plan along specific lines. For example, it may be necessary to have a marked patrol car present whenever students are entering and leaving the building, at bus arrival and departure times. It may be necessary to have a marked police car present and visible on the perimeter of a school playground to deter entry and dissuade gang members from congregating.

Where the risk to students exists from gunfire in areas adjacent to the school, "bullet drills," in which students learn to respond if shots are fired, may be necessary (Kodluboy, 1997). Figure 25, a memo to school staff, makes concrete the details of such a drill.

SCHOOL ISSUES

Vehicles and Parking Lots

When vehicles occupied by "representing" gang members become a demonstrable problem, numerous responses are available, depending upon the specific characteristics of the school campus. For those campuses with controlled access via long driveways, simply placing at the entrance a security person who makes eye contact with drivers, perhaps speaks with drivers before entry onto the campus, and conspicuously records license plate numbers often will deter potential miscreants.

Cars parked on campus are a special concern. While in some situations open, relatively uncontrolled parking lots represent little hazard, in many gang-impacted neighborhoods, grave problems may occur. Such neighborhoods should exert strict control over parking lots. A single, supervised entrance is highly recommended.

Figure 25—Sample Protocol for Gunfire and Building Intruders

To: All staff

From: Administration

Re: Protocol for gunfire and building intruders

When you hear the following over the loudspeaker, please do not leave the school building: "Attention all staff: All outdoor activities are cancelled." This means that all exterior doors will be locked and monitored. Do not attempt to leave the building or use the playground or athletic field. Normal movement within the school building may continue.

When you hear "Attention all staff: Dr. Green is in the building," this means a total building lockdown is in effect. Do not leave your classroom. Lock your door and while doing so direct any passing staff members or students to enter your room immediately. Do not allow any staff member or student to leave your classroom until you hear the "All clear" message. Do not call the office for clarification. The office will call you or issue an "All staff" call to update you.

Begin outdoor security training for your classroom. You may wish to carry a whistle. One long blast of the whistle means "Look at me and do as I do." This may be dropping to the

---

ground or remaining motionless. Three short blasts mean "Follow me now!" It is appropriate to do three successive bursts of three short blasts to be certain that all students and nearby adults can hear the directive. Do not use three whistle blasts for any other reason.

If a playground emergency occurs, follow the directions given by members of the security staff. They will be in touch with each other and the police officer on duty, so they may give you the best advice.

If you hear gunfire, do not automatically move to the school door. Stop, listen, and look! If you must act immediately, it may be best to drop to the ground until the direction and location of the gunfire are determined. We do not want three or four classrooms running to the door, serving as moving targets, if the shooting is immediately next to where the students are playing or between the students and the school door.

If the shooting is away from your position, moving to the door briskly may be the best response. If the shooting is very close to your position, dropping to the ground may be the best response. When in doubt, drop! Also, when in doubt, look to security personnel if they are available.

As you can see, each incident will probably be different and require a different response. When a police officer is present, the officer will direct the security staff and all within earshot as to the expected course of action. When only security personnel are present, they will make the call and advise you. When you are alone on the playground, take a radio and take the initiative!

If a chaotic situation occurs, personal initiative and best judgment may be your only guide.

If state and local laws allow, students who wish to park cars on school property should be required to purchase or receive parking stickers, to be permanently affixed to the vehicle window. An advisory should be printed on the sticker and a sign posted at all parking lot entrances stating that parking on school property implies consent to a "reasonable-suspicion" search of the vehicle. All requirements of what constitutes a reasonable search would then apply (National School Safety Center, 1995). Removable, multicar parking cards or hang tags are not recommended.

In high-risk neighborhoods, where local crime data support the need, the installation of security fencing is recommended. Inviting local police to conduct random, frequent police patrols of the lots during the school day and especially during critical movement times can provide an additional measure of safety in the lots.

Lockers

Maintaining control of school lockers is a relatively easy strategy for increasing school safety. Providing students and parents receive prior notice that the school maintains control of the lockers at all times, the use of random reasonable-suspicion searches is generally allowed. Along with written notice of the intent to maintain control, it is necessary to demonstrate such control by disallowing students to use personal locks or store non-school-related items in the lockers, as well as to keep documentation that students and their parents are fully advised of the district's intent. To meet the standards of a reasonable-suspicion search, it is necessary to demonstrate an articulable belief, which would be formed by a reasonable person who is knowledgeable of schools and students, that contraband is contained within the locker. A reasonable belief is one based upon what a teacher directly hears or sees, or on what is reported to the teacher by another person. The urgency and scope of the search would be limited by exactly what contraband is suspected of being in the locker and when the information is obtained. A rumor that a student was seen with a weapon in the neighborhood might preclude a reasonable-suspicion locker search on a school day a week later. Such a search would be allowed if a teacher hears from a reliable person that a student has a gun in school today; the teacher observes a large, heavy object in the student's coat; and other students report that they also have seen the student with a weapon. Simply put, if a reasonable person would believe that the student possesses significant contraband on the school day in question, the student and locker may be searched without interfering with the student's Fourth Amendment rights (National School Safety Center, 1995). Random searches of all lockers are also permissible with prior notification of students and parents that such searches may occur at any time during the school year.

The Open Campus

Restricting student movement by closing the campus is highly controversial but highly cost effective. By preventing student movement in and out of the school during the school day, officials can reduce staff time spent monitoring entrances and exits. Such policies can also prevent the entrance of intruders and reduce risk to students who might otherwise leave campus at noon for lunch at local student gathering spots. While districts do not commonly highlight such problems, we are aware of situations in which students who left high-school campuses for lunch or to go home to retrieve forgotten school materials have been shot, stabbed, or beaten by gang members in the community. While a closed campus cannot prevent such occurrences before or after school, they can at least reduce one such exposure to violence during the school day.

When suspected gang members, especially those who are not students, attempt to enter campus, they should be queried by security to determine their reason for being on campus. Known status of a visitor as a gang member, the presence of gang tattoos, display of gang colors, and gang hand signs or gang speech should alert security staff and campus greeters that it is necessary to speak to the visitor. If the school has a policy prohibiting gang displays on campus—based on past provable instances of major disruption to the safety and mission of the school or due to gang-related behavior—it may be possible to forbid entry to persons engaging in such gang displays. It may be useful to seek trespass notices or other court orders to prohibit the entry to campus of individuals who, because of gang-related behavior, represent a clear and present danger to the mission of the school. Careful consultation with school district attorneys should inform school personnel as to lawful implementation of such policies and legal status in their jurisdiction.

Drive-by Decisions

Commonly, schools are located on public thoroughfares, where controlled access is difficult at best. Some school districts—Pittsburgh among them—have achieved a measure of control at selected sites by gaining city and neighborhood support for blocking streets with removable barricades during morning arrival and afternoon dismissal times. Other possibilities to reduce, slow, or redirect traffic involve engagement of city and community support. Posting of no-parking signs along vulnerable areas, adding stop signs, lowering speed limits, increasing presence of police traffic patrols, adding speed bumps on secondary streets, and installing traffic diversion barriers that reroute high vehicle-count traffic onto selected streets all allow for greater traffic control, thus reducing or preventing gang congregation, drive-by altercations, and intimidation. Such controls also give police officers a legal tool to engage persons present on campus who harbor ill-intent, should they violate the traffic laws.

While "walk-up" and "bike-up" shootings do occur, most planned gang incidents involving guns on campus also involve arrival or departure by one or more cars. Safety staff should note that it is not uncommon for two cars to be involved in a drive-by shooting, with the first being the "call-out" car and the second being the "shooter" car. The call-out car occupants engage the potential victims in gang displays and counterdisplays of insults and gang hand signs. When the victims are in unobstructed view, the occupants of the second, shooter car pull up and open fire.

Physical Characteristics of a Safe Campus Perimeter

The announcement of the construction of a new school is often greeted with neighborhood concerns about increased traffic, loss of street parking to student drivers, and the presence of teenage youth in the neighborhood. Architects and others struggle with competing interests to design a building and campus to meet many diverse needs. Increasingly, a safety consultant is an active participant in the design or remodeling of a school. Balancing the desire for a visually inviting structure with the need to keep the campus safe is difficult at best. Often, one need or desire appears to outweigh the other as final plans are drawn. While the perfect design may be an unattainable goal, some characteristics of a safe school may be adapted to virtually any site.

The campus itself should be viewed not only from the building out, but also from the neighborhood in. Security staff should walk the neighborhood and develop site views from nearby alleys, streets, intersections, businesses, and housing areas. Potential threats from the neighborhood and common patterns of vehicle and foot traffic, as well as sight lines, may influence the placement or monitoring of doors and surface parking lots, choice of standard or high-security windows, designation of appropriate playground areas, installation of security cameras and audible alarms, and deployment of security personnel.

Selection and proper placement of landscaping materials, construction and location of dual-service sidewalks (which allow access by police patrol cars), and placement of high- or low-intensity lighting, walls, and fences all allow for greater or lesser visual scrutiny by passersby and the police. In some instances, high-security lighting is desirable, while in other jurisdictions (e.g., some San Diego public schools), a "lights out" policy has been more effective than fixed, high-intensity lighting in reducing vandalism. What is most important is that design or remodeling of a school site be driven by educational function, safety concerns, and ease of monitoring by school staff and local law enforcement. Safety measures cannot easily be applied after brick and mortar are in place. Careful collaboration among all interested parties during initial design, major remodeling, and security reviews will allow for the most efficient and least intrusive fixed and variable security installations and deployments.

Where gunfire, hurled rocks, intimidating congregations of aggressive youth (including gang-involved youth), or repeated trespass to the campus occur along the perimeter of a school campus, physical changes must be considered. In some instances, moving a playground from one side of campus to another area, out of the line of sight of dangerous persons, will preempt intentional acts (i.e., gunfire and interpersonal challenges). Interrupting the sight lines of potential aggressors also decreases challenging responses from students, intruders' chances of identifying potential victims, reasons for intruders to enter campus, and risk to students should gunfire erupt. Doing so also increases the comfort of students who fear intimidation from outside persons.

The construction of earth berms, living visual barriers such as perimeter shrubs or trees, or solid intruder walls (sometimes locally referred to as "bullet walls") can all decrease physical risk and challenges to students during the school day (Gaustad, 1991). Close collaboration with the community before such structures are built can allay concerns that the community is being "closed out" from the school. It is also important to note that while solid barriers can decrease risks to students from outside forces during the school day, they prevent local law enforcement, community watch groups, and supportive community members from visually observing and monitoring the campus during nonschool hours.

Physical Characteristics of a Safe School Building

A single school district can include anything from 75-year-old buildings to modern architectural extravaganzas. If security measures have not been built into the structures from initial design, or retrofitted during remodeling, physical security enhancements can present particular challenges to school administrators. Assuming completion of all assessed campus perimeter security modifications, the school security officer can turn full attention to specific building adaptations.

Doors and windows provide direct access to and egress from the school building for staff, students, visitors, and criminally inclined persons. It is not uncommon for a large school serving more than 1,000 students to have dozens of exterior doors. Even a small school may have a dozen exterior doors. While in low-risk neighborhoods an unattended unlocked door or a door kept ajar for ventilation may lead to nothing of concern, more serious problems can also occur. School staff members may encounter youthful burglars wandering a building, rattling doors during the school day, looking for an open classroom. Such persons typically enter unlocked classrooms, head directly for the teacher's desk, and often find a teacher's purse or other valuables in the lower right-hand drawer.

Laptop computers are also a frequent target of both daytime and after-hours intruders. It is common for a staff member to confront such intruders, sometimes in the act of theft, but to assume that the person is simply lost and legitimately looking for some other staff member. At this moment, even in low-risk neighborhoods, the risk of physical danger to the confronting staff member is high. It is best at these times for the staff member to offer direction calmly, and, only if the staff member feels safe doing so, escort or direct the intruder to the office or the nearest exit door. A prompt call to the office for security assistance is always the best next action for the person discovering the intruder. If an intruder is caught in the act of committing a property crime, the staff member should concentrate on identifying, rather than apprehending, the intruder. Heroics are best left to trained security staff.

In a high-risk, gang-impacted neighborhood, leaving doors unlocked or ajar increases the risk of theft by burglary and of encountering congregations of gang-involved youth entering or wandering through the school. Confronting gang-involved intruders is at best an uncomfortable and, on occasion, decidedly dangerous step. Clearly, each building in a gang-impacted neighborhood must have an unequivocal policy about closing and locking doors and windows. If the building safety officer determines there is a risk of entry to the building by gang members or others who have no legitimate purpose in being on campus, a locked door and window policy should be mandatory.

Depending upon the assessed likelihood of entry and the degree of threat from such entry, a proportionate response can be made. In low- to medium-risk schools, simply locking all doors and windows between hours of assessed risk may be sufficient. In such schools, staff must be informed of the degree of risk and potential consequences to staff and students should doors or windows be left unlocked. Security or other staff should check and secure doors and windows following times when they are likely to be left open (i.e., during arrival and dismissal). At other times during the day, random door checks are advised. At no time should a door be left ajar, such as when tradespersons are making repeated trips into the building with deliveries or equipment, unless a security person is available to monitor the door. Although schools are required by local fire codes to have all doors available for immediate egress, usually by use of "panic bars," the unrestricted use of such doors may allow the entry of gang members and others as legitimate visitors exit the building. Staff leaving a building by a secure door must follow a policy of not allowing entry by any person who does not have school district identification. Even parents must enter and exit the building by doors monitored by security staff, security cameras, or voice identification security intercoms. A parent, staff member, or other visitor who leaves the building by an unmonitored locked exit is unwittingly giving intruders, including gang members, the opportunity to gain entry.

It is important to reinforce constantly the need to keep doors and easily entered ground-level windows locked. Individual staff members often will attempt to justify their violation of virtually any locked window and door policy. Poor ventilation, dislike of showing mistrust for others, personal freedom, convenience, and countless other reasons explain laxness in abiding by safety procedures. None of these reasons is an excuse for a security lapse, and none should be accepted by administration, fellow staff, students, or parents. Staff training and ongoing monitoring and encouragement are necessary to ensure adherence.

For designated, frequently used entrances and exits, as well as for doors that are at high risk for illegal entry, the use of magnetic locks and video cameras is highly recommended. For maximum electronic security, the addition of alternating or sequencing cameras, along with time-lapse video recording equipment, is highly desirable. Magnetic locks prevent exit from doors except with an override key, as when the fire alarm system has been activated or when there is a complete building power failure. These devices dramatically decrease the use of protected doors as unauthorized exits or entrances. While magnetic locks can be overcome from the inside with extreme force, they are nonetheless an excellent building security enhancement. High-risk doors can also be outfitted with annunciators. An annunciator is a lighted visual and/or audible warning on a central security panel, activated whenever a monitored door is opened.

Closed circuit cameras are excellent deterrent devices, which allow monitoring of controlled access to the building. Monitors are generally mounted near the security desk, if present, or at a desk in the main office building, where they are supervised by clerical personnel. The person monitoring the desk can admit an approved visitor simply by pressing a button that momentarily releases the magnetic lock.

For true high-risk settings, the installation of multiple-camera, time-lapse video systems is highly desirable. Such systems record several seconds of tape from each camera on the system, in a fixed or random pattern. The best systems have multiple monitors so staff can continuously monitor a single area of concern while a main screen continues to provide brief, sequential images of all monitored areas. Should a prohibited entry or criminal act occur within range of a camera, the probability of recording the act is greatly enhanced. If gang members are recorded engaging in illegal entry or any other activity while they are wearing gang colors, displaying gang hand signs, or committing graffiti vandalism, district discipline procedures may be invoked, and law enforcement may be engaged if a criminal act has occurred. Successful administrative and law enforcement intervention is far more likely when the event is recorded on tape than if no adult witnesses, or if eyewitness-only accounts, are available.

In high-risk buildings, it may be necessary to carefully assess the building for blind spots, unlocked empty rooms, unmonitored stairwells, and cul-de-sac hallways. Any physical space that cannot be regularly observed by passing staff and security officers should be secured from student access. Student toilets are a special concern. When students are drawn from highly disorganized neighborhoods and when there is a high gang presence in a school, physical intimidation by gang members, gang graffiti vandalism, drug sales or use, and brandishing of weapons are common in student toilets, as well as in other areas. Well-lighted toilets, randomly entered by security and other staff, are essential to provide for student safety. Immediate removal of any gang graffiti from such areas is important to decrease the intimidation factor for nongang or rival gang students.

Metal Detectors

The use of metal detectors at restricted building points is controversial, especially when such efforts are misapplied or if the community has not been actively involved in the implementation of a weapons detection strategy (Harrington-Lueker, 1992; National League of Cities, 1994). Metal detectors and physical searches often are last resorts, best applied when building, neighborhood, perimeter, and community strategies are already in place. The National League of Cities reports that, of 700 cities surveyed, 133 school districts now use metal detectors on some occasions. It is necessary to work closely with the school district's attorneys before implementing a metal detection policy, due to differences in local laws.

Basically, metal detectors may be used either on a fixed, permanent or on a random, situation-specific basis. When a security assessment indicates a high risk of weapons entry into a building, a fixed, walk-through metal detector, perhaps along with hand-held detectors, may be desirable. The school administrator may require all students and visitors to pass through the detector or use a truly random, time-based paradigm to stop individuals entering the school. To otherwise select individuals without a clearly articulated reason risks violation of an individual's right to freedom from unreasonable search or seizure. In most jurisdictions, to conduct a search the administration must have a reasonable suspicion that an individual is carrying contraband that represents a clear and present danger to student and staff safety or to the general order and achievement of the school's mission. The suspicion must be clearly articulated in order to conduct individual searches. These searches are generally limited in scope to jackets, purses, bookbags, and the like (Gaustad, 1991; Harrington-Lueker, 1992; National Association of School Safety and Law Enforcement Officers, 1994).

While utilizing metal detectors may at first cause significant discomfort for students, parents, staff, and the greater community, such concerns usually can be allayed. Doing so requires careful planning involving all interested and concerned stakeholders, including students. Implementing other less intrusive and proactive prevention and intervention strategies must precede, or at least be concurrent with, use of a metal detection strategy.

See-through Barriers

Most controversial and often quite troubling for a school community is the suggestion that some schools in high-risk neighborhoods use bullet-resistant glass or high-security bullet-resistant screens on doors and windows. Few districts discuss such installations publicly, thus making related decision variables unavailable for debate. It appears likely that with proper attention to all other measures discussed in this chapter, such installations will rarely be needed. Only in the most dangerous neighborhoods, where other control strategies have been faithfully implemented and the data continue to suggest high risk to persons inside the school from gunfire outside the school, will such installations be important.

It is difficult at best to determine such risks prior to the occurrence of indicator events in the community. Obvious events include a history of gunfire toward the school, of persons fleeing gunfire while attempting to enter the school, of repeated credible threats of firearms assaults made toward students or staff, or of continuing gunfire incidents in the neighborhood immediately adjacent to the school. Should such events be unresponsive to other intensive prevention and intervention strategies, the district may wish to install bullet-resistant windows in select locations.

WITHIN-BUILDING PROCEDURES

Graffiti

It is imperative to implement and monitor a zero-tolerance policy toward gang and other graffiti. When gang graffiti are present, it is only a matter of time until tagger graffiti appear. Graffiti vandalism degrades school climate; results in student fear and rejection of the school as a safe, controlled environment; and often leads to physical confrontations among students. It is important to remove all graffiti as soon as it is observed and noted and to refer to graffiti as "graffiti vandalism" rather than "graffiti art." According to local codes, a student caught damaging surfaces with graffiti may be ticketed for vandalism by the school liaison officer or local law enforcement officer. Following parent notification of the student's commission of any significant act of graffiti vandalism, the student may be required to make restitution through money or work. Many schools send parents a list of school supplies needed each fall or semester. This list also should include prohibited items and consequences for their possession. Often-prohibited items include permanent markers, etching tools, and spray containers. When a legitimate use for such materials exists (e.g., in an art class), the school may elect to provide and monitor their use within a supervised environment. For advanced students, a sign-out policy for such materials may be instituted.

It is not recommended to allow special walls, bulletin boards, or other displays of graffiti. Such efforts generally backfire because they legitimize graffiti and graffiti style. Often the graffiti increase, if not in school, then in areas adjacent to and on student travel routes. Graffiti vandals who possess artistic talent generally are limited in their skill and expression to graffiti-style painting. Because of the limited and declining acceptance of this style, it is a disservice to encourage such students to develop the graffiti style. A better course is to help them add more conventional and respected art techniques to their repertoires and to encourage alternative forms of expression. Helping students become better vandals is not a goal of education.

Graffiti are found on student notebooks, assignment sheets, desks, backpacks, hats (especially under the brim), clothing, shoes, books, computer printed assignments, toilet walls, and elsewhere. Vigilance and yearly graffiti training updates are essential for staff.

Student Movement

Control over student movement is dictated by numerous variables, including degree of threat, if any, from the adjacent neighborhood; threat from contentious interactions among disparate student groups, especially rival gangs; overall culture of the school, including staff and student interactions and relationships; training and educational orientation of staff; students' home and neighborhood culture, age, and maturity; the physical plan of the school; lighting, both ambient (from windows) and electric; staff-student ratio; and administrative leadership style.

In low-threat buildings, student movement is controlled by the width of corridors, the visible presence of a few staff, a brief but reasonable length of time for transitions, the clear designation of areas in which students may congregate (e.g., student lounge or commons), and by rules for individual and small-group student movement during the day (necessitated by multiple within-building and off-campus program activities).

Medium-threat buildings require greater control over campus and building movement, a higher number of staff visible during all large-group student movements, limited movement times during the day, limited and supervised areas where student congregation is allowed, increased use of specifically designated and identifiable security staff, controlled access to campus for all persons, and a formal communication system for staff to access support personnel immediately. The school should review the need for staff and student picture identification badges, and student access to nonstaffed areas of the school may need to be restricted.

High-threat buildings are generally within or adjacent to high-threat neighborhoods, where instances of violence are common. When such schools draw from the immediate and one or more distant neighborhoods, the risk of conflict increases, and therefore a greater need to control student movement exists. Building access should be monitored by radio-equipped security staff and administration during high-risk arrival and departure times, as well as throughout the school day. It is desirable to have uniformed police officers present on campus, at least from the lunch hour to the departure of buses at the end of the school day. Other measures advised include staff and student picture identification badges; a formal pass system with strong enforcement; high staff-student ratios; elimination of bookbags, purses, and the like; increased lighting and improvement of sight lines through removal of physical barriers; and closing off travel through some areas. All visitors should wear identification badges of some type, controlled by the office or security staff.

Dress Codes

Dress codes are an increasingly lively topic and at times a contentious and divisive issue for staff and students. Kodluboy (1997) Kodluboy and Evenrud (1993), J. Burke (1991), N.D. Burke (1993), and Evenrud (1997) have commented upon the issues to be addressed when implementing a dress code policy. Numerous court cases—such as *Oleson v. Board of Education* (1987), *Tinker v. Des Moines* (1969), and *Bethel v. Fraser* (1986)—provide instruction to school officials who are considering a school dress code. (Table 7 in chapter 2 lists items frequently proscribed by dress codes.)

Forums for discussion of uniforms and dress codes differ depending on the constituencies involved: staff, parents, and students. Parents and teachers often discuss their concerns through a parent-teacher organization or planned community meetings. Students generally express their concerns regarding dress directly to their parents and through student council representation and other school and community forums. All stakeholders then engage in discussion of the desirability of adopting a dress code or uniform policy.

While gang activity is often mentioned at least obliquely in discussions of dress codes or uniforms, the general focus usually is on eliminating an expensive and distracting clothes orientation among students. When a dress code suggesting or requiring school uniforms is discussed, decreased expense of uniforms as compared to expensive, designer-name clothing is highlighted. Few data are available to guide the administrator in such matters. The move to uniforms is more a function of community consensus than a databased decision. It has been suggested in this context that, in addition to discouraging the wearing of gang-signifying attire, school uniforms discourage clothing theft, reduce invidious comparisons of appearance, and enhance the school population's sense of community.

The move to formal dress codes is a more deliberate and information-based decision. N.D. Burke (1993), Kodluboy and Evenrud (1993), and Evenrud (1997) have identified basic issues to consider when implementing a dress code. The first and most important issue is the reason for suggesting a dress code. Dress codes that prohibit certain hairstyles or specific articles of clothing as a matter of taste or administrative preference should not be disguised as matters of safety. Nor should dress codes be hastily implemented as a disproportionate response to single events occurring in the community (e.g., thefts of starter jackets).

The function of a dress code is to maintain or enhance student safety and, to a less well-studied degree, to improve academic achievement. When an entire school community—including parents, students, and school officials—agree to implement a dress code through a collective, deliberative, inclusive process, few challenges to the policy are likely to occur. When the policy is driven by the school administration, the decision may be challenged, and the administration may be required to provide justification. The most common and defensible justification for implementing a dress code is the observation, as provable fact, that the display of a specific manner of dress has resulted in a substantial disruption of the school environment. For example, the administration may have documented that persons who wear blue bandanas hanging from the right rear pants pocket consistently fight with individuals who wear red bandanas hanging from the left rear pants pocket. In this example, concerning conflict between Gangster Disciples and Vice Lords, bandanas may be prohibited in the school.

As mentioned, a dress code should be narrowly drawn, based on instances of provable fact. The code is designed to maintain physical safety, not to prohibit otherwise protected speech. In addition, the code must recognize differences in students' age and maturity while serving the purpose of educating students. A gang-prohibitive dress code is an important contribution to the safety of a school in that instances of disruption, intimidation, and aggression can be reduced, if not eliminated.

Developing a rational dress code that can withstand legal challenges may be done by (a) utilizing incident documentation forms to provide relevant facts, (b) collaborating in legally permissible information exchanges with local gang unit police officers, (c) sharing investigative information between schools when gang activity occurs, (d) documenting and reviewing graffiti trends along with other visible and audible forms of gang representing, and (e) interviewing gang-involved students and communicating with parents and other community members. These actions will allow school staff to develop a list of safety concerns relating to dress, as well as to graffiti, language, and gestures. Should these specific and limited behaviors be shown by past incidents of articulable fact to have resulted in fights, increased truancy of fearful students, teacher assaults, student assaults, and similar substantial and material disruptions to the educational process, prohibition of their display on campus is likely permissible (N.D. Burke, 1993). Careful review of the dress code by local authorities, school attorneys, and parent and student groups is highly encouraged. Such reviews may decrease resistance, increase compliance, and decrease legal challenges.

STAFF SELECTION AND TRAINING

Administrative and Teaching Staff

While selection of administrators and teachers is generally highly circumscribed by contractual obligations, acceptance or rejection criteria tied to specific educational reasons are generally allowed. If a school is located in a highly gang-impacted neighborhood, and if it will be necessary for staff to engage many gang-involved students, it is appropriate to emphasize certain conditions of employment. Administrative and teaching staff must be knowledgeable about the ethnic backgrounds of students, know the difference between ethnic-cultural variables and gang-subcultural variables (Kodluboy, 1994; Kodluboy & Evenrud, 1993), learn the specific gang practices in the school attendance areas, be respectful of all students and their families, show calm during crisis, be resistant to both subtle and blatant intimidation efforts of gang-involved students, be dedicated to the academic and social potential of all students (irrespective of their gang involvement), be intolerant of any displays of gang iden-tification or gang subcultural values, avoid interactions with gang-involved students that are stereotypical rather than individual, and be highly resistant to stress or at least able to recover quickly and focus on students' academic and social growth.

While some have suggested that staff-student interactions with gang members are somehow qualitatively different from those with other students, we find differently. It is educationally inappropriate and certainly counterproductive to rudely or publicly demean a student's gang identification; it is equally inappropriate to disrespect any aspect of a student's life, and this is especially true for students living a marginal existence. Both gang-involved students and many other marginal, nongang students dislike and react negatively to being publicly singled out. Indeed, reacting to such students in a stereotypical, rigid manner is likely to make problems worse. Pre-determined responses to gang-involved students may only reinforce their identity as gang members and make transition to a more normal existence even more difficult. It is best to take a respectful, individual approach to interactions with gang members, focusing on actions and not an abstract concept of what gang members are or how gang members might react. Setting the stage for, expecting, and reinforcing the conventional attributes of students' behavior will result in greater gains and fewer problem behaviors than will treating them all as dangerous, reactive youth. Administrators and teachers who cannot adopt such an attitude might best be employed in a less exacting setting.

Support Staff

Selecting support staff, such as educational assistants, is usually far easier than selecting administrators or teachers in that job descriptions are narrower and prescribed interactions with students are more directly under the observation of supervisory staff. Nonetheless, it is necessary for support staff to exhibit the same general attributes described for teachers and administrators.

It is in hiring security staff that the greatest challenge lies. Each building or district must adopt basic standards for security staff requirements, training, and supervision. Minimum requirements should include a criminal background check, as allowed by current state and local laws; drug screening, referenced to current state and local laws; and completion of minimum basic training, including first-responder medical training and problem deescalation training. Applicants should also receive training by qualified instructors in the appropriate use of force, limits on possession and use of allowable equipment (e.g., handcuffs, mace), local laws and ordinances regarding schools and the school campus (including trespass laws), limits on school staff when conducting search and seizure, radio procedures, when to call 911, and when to notify administration. Security staff must be licensed and bonded or likewise indemnified by the school district. It is highly recommended that security staff be subject to a condition of employment that prohibits fraternization with students during or outside of the school day (Kodluboy, 1997; Kodluboy & Evenrud, 1993). It is also imperative for the district to develop written policy with appropriate due process protections for refusing employment or terminating employment of individuals proven to engage in behavior incompatible with the mission of the school district (Trump, 1997), in this instance, gang-related criminal behavior. All such policies must be consistent with employment law.

A major decision for school districts is what model to select for deployment of security staff. Districts may elect to develop a specific job description for security officers and directly hire and train their own personnel. Because most school districts are self-insured, possession of a license and bond may or may not be a minimum requirement. In this case, it is important to follow the recommendations of district legal counsel.

Some districts may elect to hire a security firm to provide individual officers for specific buildings. If such a choice is made, district legal counsel must conduct a thorough background check of the provider, including review of and fidelity of implementing hiring criteria, a search for complaint histories, a search for legal actions taken against the firm, and on-site visits to any other school district that employs the firm.

While differences of opinion exist regarding security staff uniforms, at the very least, designated security staff should follow a strict dress code so they are easily differentiated from other personnel. Blue jeans, tennis shoes, logo T-shirts, and the like will not engender respect from students, parents, or intruders. A professional demeanor is facilitated by professional dress.

As mentioned, security personnel must learn and use standard radio procedures and terminology. The radio is the basic communications link between security officers and the central office and administration. While some districts elect to employ basic radio codes, it is generally sufficient to instruct staff to use brief messages, avoid using student names, avoid unnecessary commentary or discussion, refrain from using the radio as a tool for personal discussions, and never permit students to handle the radio.

As noted earlier, a sometimes contentious issue is whether to allow or disallow the hiring of former gang members as security staff. In general it is preferable to hire highly gang-informed individuals who have not been gang members. It is recommended that former gang members be hired only if their gang life is far behind them and if they have received or are willing to complete appropriate training and subject themselves to close supervision. Former gang members who have completed or are attending college, served successfully in the military, held steady employment for some extended period of time, are settled in the community, disavow current connection with a gang, and/or are active in conventional community activities are far preferable to those who exhibit fewer indicators that they are indeed former, not active or dormant, gang members (Kodluboy & Evenrud, 1993). Students deserve better role models than current gang members as security officers.

As was found in the New York experience and described at length in chapter 6, current gang membership is often incompatible with the role of security officer. Adult gang members have often sworn an oath to treat fellow gang members differentially and to maintain loyalty to their fellow gang members, at best a conflict of interest. No data suggest that hiring currently active gang members or gang leaders as security personnel, mediators, or in any other similar capacity is desirable (Kodluboy, 1997; Kodluboy & Evenrud, 1993). Should a district choose to or feel compelled to hire former, or even current, gang members as security staff, it is critical to inform them that any gang-related behavior, any gang display, or any differential treatment of gang members versus nongang students is in violation of the district's zero-tolerance standards and may be grounds for appropriate discipline. Due process and an appeals procedure should be established by attorneys for the district, for the protection of employees accused of such behavior.

The best-qualified applicants for many security positions are generally active or retired police officers. Such individuals have extensive training and experience, know all relevant law, provide outstanding deterrence, and garner the highest respect from interested persons.

These attributes of course make them the most expensive choice. A cost-benefit analysis will determine their value to the district in high-risk locations. If the school is in a dangerous locale and if gang conflicts are common, hiring licensed police officers may be a bargain. Because budgets often are inadequate to hire more than one officer per site, it may be appropriate to deploy one sworn officer and several, non-sworn security persons. Such differentiated staffing may provide the best overall safety coverage. Districts may employ several other models, such as the use of police liaison officers, or active on-duty police officers paid by the school district. Police in some cities are assigned to patrol districts and handle all reports and investigations in the schools located in those districts. Any model chosen must be based upon data, community input, and school interests and needs. In addition, it should be subject to yearly review (Trump, 1997).

EMERGENCY RESPONSES

In the past, emergency preparation focused primarily on planning for fires and natural phenomena such as earthquakes, tornadoes, or blizzards. Intruders have become a concern in the recent past, causing some districts to lock school doors and perhaps place greeters at the school's entrance to direct visitors to the office. Sadly, schools now commonly face threats from armed intruders, gunfire adjacent to the school, and students who bring weapons to school. In this light, many districts now require written school safety plans and have designated district-level school safety or loss prevention officers (Stephens, 1997; Trump, 1997). These individuals are responsible for assisting building-level administrators with training and execution of school safety plans.

A school safety plan is a written document specifying emergencies that have occurred or are likely to occur in the school district, including natural phenomena (e.g., flood, blizzard, tornado, earthquake, etc.), environmental phenomena (e.g., fire, gas leak, power failure, structural failure, etc.), intruder trouble (e.g., nonstudent gang members, threatening or hostile visitors, nonstudent demonstrators, etc.), and threats adjacent to the school (e.g., civil unrest, demonstrations, gunfire, police searches, etc.).

Commonly, the plan is contained in a school safety manual, indexed by topic for quick reference. Each emergency action plan is written in simple sentence-outline form. Bold headings introduce each step of the action plan. Each action plan designates personnel by name and describes their particular task or series of tasks when responding to specific emergencies. Follow-up activities are included for implementation when the emergency has passed—for example, sending form letters to update parents, administration, and, if appropriate, the media as to the nature of the emergency, its impact on the school, the outcome of the emergency, and future steps to be taken by the school should such action be suggested by the outcome. The plan is reviewed by district-level officials, who are responsible for loss prevention and emergency response, as well as by school board attorneys. In addition, it is presented to staff each fall during teacher training.

The school safety plan provides each individual in the school with action steps for all reasonably foreseeable emergencies, thus allowing staff to proceed in an orderly manner. Anticipating emergencies allows for planning proportional responses and makes explaining or justifying actions taken relatively easy and comprehensive. Planning also conveys to parents and the community that school personnel are thoughtful and competent to protect and educate their children. Acting in a swift, proportional, competent manner alleviates students' fears rather than generating mistrust and anxiety. Planning for emergencies is far easier and more cost effective than is explaining a poor response to an emergency, especially if there is a tragic consequence as a result. School staff must always be prepared to state that all that could be anticipated was anticipated and all that could be done was done.

SPECIAL EVENTS

Special events require particular consideration when gang activity is expected or has occurred in the past. For open-air events, such as football games, it is essential to provide the visible presence of uniformed police and security officers. Security is further enhanced by the presence of school staff who are wearing clearly visible identification badges and, in the case of some, carrying communication radios. Having parked squad cars visible to persons driving past the event is desirable, as is the use of frequent "roll-bys" by patrol cars from the police jurisdiction in which the event is being held. Walk-through metal detectors may be justified when a threat of weapons or a history of weapons possession and use exists and when entrances are well-controlled and limited. Prior notification of attendees from all involved schools that gang representing is prohibited on school property is advised. Such a notice should be on all advertising for the event and on any tickets distributed for admission. Persons who represent may be prohibited entry should they constitute an articulable threat of disruption during the school event.

The use of plainclothes security or police officers in either public or hidden observation posts is sometimes appropriate in high-risk situations. Such officers, perhaps hidden in a high place adjacent to the entrance of an event, may use binoculars to spot individuals and groups engaging in questionable behavior. It is important that such officers know the student body or at least the local gang culture so they may anticipate gang conflicts.

Staff-student ratios should be determined by the specific circumstance before a final decision is made to hold an event. If students from other schools are allowed to attend an event such as a dance, they must have that school's current photo ID. If they have none, they may be refused entrance. If student interaction at the event will be high and the physical area small and with poor visibility, such as at a dance with a small dance floor, there must be a high staff-student ratio. If the interaction will be low, the area is large, and visibility is good, such as at a daytime football game, the ratio may be lower.

SUMMARY

Controlling the school environment can be as simple as locking a few doors and meeting with a small number of students and their parents to agree to leave all gang representing out of the school. Controlling the school can also involve intensive security patrols, metal detectors, tight supervision, and strict control of student movement. For most schools, the issues officials, teachers, and students face are somewhere in between. What is important is that each district adopt a best-practice, databased approach to developing a comprehensive security plan. Each district should carefully follow trends occurring in adjacent districts and nearby cities with similar demographics. Most important is that district officials try to avoid the complacency that marks the past experience of most cities and school districts when gang violence first appears. A proportionate, considered response early in the evolution of the gang presence will help prevent more serious problems on down the line. If educators can agree with their colleagues, administration, parents, the community, and the school board that it is better to plan ahead than it is to apologize for not being prepared, all are served.

CHAPTER EIGHT

In-School & Community Enrichment Solutions

As noted in chapter 6, comprehensiveness is a crucial feature of the gang prevention and intervention programming initiative. In the many ways suggested in chapter 7, a comprehensive plan for maximizing school safety must be formulated and carried out. But successful gang prevention and intervention require considerably more than efforts to control and contain. Of equal and perhaps greater potential value are efforts to enrich. Schools and communities must creatively extend themselves to "sweeten" the school and after-school day—to make conventional choices constructive and fulfilling for gang youth, for wanabees, for potentials, for everyone.

In a real sense, youths often join gangs for enrichment purposes. As discussed in chapter 3, gang membership is seen as meeting normal, healthy adolescent needs, including friendship, pride, self-esteem, identity development, excitement, and more. Can schools and communities meet these same needs in a more prosocial and less damaging manner, even for a minority of gang-attracted youth? We think so, and in the present chapter will describe a number of enriching school and community gang prevention and intervention programs and strategies.

A similar perspective on the need for enrichment is offered by Csikszentmihalyi and Larsen (1978) in their enjoyment theory of school violence. As noted in chapter 1, they suggest that in-school vandalism may grow in substantial part from students' sense that their school experiences are boring, irrelevant to current needs or future plans, and an inadequate match to the talents and skills students feel they do possess:

> An activity seems to be enjoyable when a person perceives that his or her capacity to act (or skills) match the opportunities for action perceived in the environment (or challenges). In this balanced state of interaction—which appears to be the subjective counterpart of the optimal arousal state—people find themselves in a peculiar dynamic experience which we have called the flow state. (p. 13)

In these authors' view, flow is impeded—and boredom encouraged—when activities lack graduated challenge, predictability, feedback, and clear goals. For many youths, especially those who find schools lacking in these qualities,

> violent confrontations provide the most clearly understood match between challenges and skills, the clearest goals, the most immediate feedback. It is for this reason, presumably, that so many young children's flow experiences involve violent or destructive acts. Children who learn no other skills or see no other opportunities for action find violence and destruction a ready source of enjoyment. . . . Unfortunately, school activities often fail to provide flow experiences, so students do not get intrinsically motivated to take part in them. (pp. 18–19)

Indeed, Csikszentmihalyi, Larsen, and Prescott (1977) found that teenage students rated themselves as more bored in school than in any other setting. Mayers (1977) found only 40% of the classes near the optimum level of balance between the challenges presented and the youths' skills.

Schools have relied heavily on technological solutions to the problem of violent behavior: alarms, lighting, fencing, and the like. In what is an apt warning, Csikszentmihalyi et al. (1977) suggest that more and more high schools are becoming mechanical systems ruled by constraints on timing, location, and behavior. The similarity between schools and jails is becoming ever more pronounced. In such a system, for many students the only way to experience the self-determining state necessary for enjoyment is to disrupt its rules. (p. 23)

Alternatively, it is desirable that schools seek a better match between challenges and skills, and thus encourage more intrinsically enjoyable participation. We believe the array of school and community programming next described provides just such a pool of intrinsically motivating, enriching, and often enjoyable growth and participation opportunities for gang members and potential gang members.

IN-SCHOOL ENRICHMENT PROGRAMMING

Programs that make the school day more meaningful and enjoyable and at the same time have their intended educational impact are best planned or selected in collaboration with the students to whom they will be targeted, delivered to the extent feasible in an individualized manner, and offered with teachers' expectancies for program success.

Collaborative Program Planning

In chapter 1 we referred briefly to collaborative or appreciative curricular development, in which topics and materials are selected and revised in consultation with persons—especially students, but also parents and others—representing diverse cultural groups and social classes. Cartledge and Johnson (1997) comment in this regard:

Within schools, students need to feel welcomed and valued, and they should be given the opportunity to develop a sense of competence, usefulness, and belonging. Passive educational climates tend to dominate our schools; students are expected to keep quiet, be attentive, and follow the teacher's directions. This atmosphere may be conducive to certain types of school performance, particularly rote learning, but does little to help a learner become an active participant in the schooling process. (p. 411)

We are not proposing that teachers give up the reins, only that they loosen them, now and then allowing a student's hand upon them along with their own. The beneficial consequences of collaborative program selection and development are not merely hoped-for outcomes. We and others have clearly demonstrated such consequences with gang-attracted youth in school settings (Goldstein & McGinnis, 1997) and with long-term gang members in community contexts (Goldstein et al., 1994). In both settings, we have provided Aggression Replacement Training (Goldstein et al., 1998), one major component of which seeks to teach youths an extended curriculum of social skills for use in everyday challenging situations (i.e., Skillstreaming). In implementing social skills instruction, we have employed a process we describe as "negotiating the curriculum":

Many of the youths for whom Skillstreaming is appropriate chronically ascribe responsibility for their antisocial acts to others. They externalize; rarely is something their fault. . . . A teacher or parent may indicate on the Skillstreaming Checklist that the youngster seldom or almost never uses two or three dozen of the prosocial skills listed. Yet the youth checks but a few of the skills as deficient! However inaccurate and inadequate such a self-picture may be, knowledge by the trainer of those few, self-admitted trainee deficiencies is golden. Teaching these skills (in addition to those that are trainer selected) has proven to be an especially positive facilitator of trainee motivation.

In what might be called a "consumer model," we give the "customer" what he or she feels is needed. The customer then much more eagerly returns to our store. Thus, as frequently as every other Skillstreaming session for any given group, we begin the meeting not by announcing and enacting a modeling display for a skill chosen by the trainers but, instead, with "How is it going?" or "What's been happening to you all since our last meeting?" Out of the brief discussion such openings engender often comes information about difficulties at home, in school, on the street, or elsewhere—difficulties that can be ameliorated or resolved by the Skillstreaming skill the trainers and trainees then jointly select and portray. The earlier in the group's life such negotiation of the curriculum commences the better. In fact, in the group's very first session, when open discussion of life difficulties by trainees may still be uncomfortable, the trainer can initiate such negotiation by tallying on a chalkboard the skills checked on the Skillstreaming Checklist by all the members of the group, without revealing who checked which ones, and then by teaching the one or ones checked most often. (Goldstein & McGinnis, 1997, pp. 25–26)

We urge teachers and other school personnel to seek other means of communicating to students both the spirit and substance of a collaborative, appreciative perspective.

Individualized Instruction

The notion of tailoring the content of instructional materials and their manner of delivery is certainly not a new one. It has appeared in many guises since public education came into being in the United States more than a century ago. Nonetheless, for the vast majority of school-age children, instruction in school is anything but individualized. Good and Brophy (1987) observe:

With the industrial revolution and the shift of population to the cities, schools became larger and education became more standardized and formalized. Age grouping became the basis for assigning students to classes, curriculum guidelines and standards were established for each grade level, and teachers began working with commercial textbooks and texts. Certain common practices for organizing and managing instruction in the public schools became well established and have continued since then as the traditional model of classroom teaching: the lock-step curriculum with its grade-level sequencing, division of the school day into periods for teaching different subject matter . . . group pacing, in which the whole class is moved through the same curriculum at roughly the same pace using largely the same materials and methods, and whole-class instructional methods, in which the teacher typically begins a lesson by reviewing prerequisite material, then introduces and develops new concepts or skills, then leads the group in a recitation or supervised practice or application activity, and then assigns seatwork or homework for students to do on their own. (p. 353)

Such a standardized philosophy and approach to educational instruction may serve many students well, but clearly it also serves many poorly. One size does not fit all. And a great many of those for whom such traditional educational practices seem to be inadequate are the marginalized, minority, lower socioeconomic youth making up the majority of youth gang membership today. A number of educational practitioners and researchers have responded to the call for more individualized instructional means, demanded by the failure of nonindividualized education. Mastery Learning (Carroll, 1963) was one early approach of this type; its central goal was to provide for individual differences in the time needed by different students to achieve mastery of a given curriculum. Adaptive Education (Walberg, 1985) went beyond individualizing time needed for learning to occur to introduce alternative methods and materials to help students learn. Programmed instruction was a popular expression of this approach. Several other individualized learning systems emerged: the Personalized System of Instruction (Keller, 1968), Individually Prescribed Instruction (Glaser & Rosner, 1975), the Program for Learning in Accordance with Need (Flanagan, Shanner, Brudner, & Marker, 1973), Individually Guided Education (Klausmeir, Rossmiller, & Saily, 1977), the Primary Education Project (Wang, 1981), and the aptitude-treatment interaction approach of Cronbach and Snow (1977). Each of these attempts to better fit methods and materials to qualities of the learner has experienced implementation problems—of staffing, materials, delivery, and, more generally, of being integrated into the practices of traditional schooling. But each has made an important statement. Education will often fail in its goals if "one size fits all" is its prevailing philosophy. For hard-to-reach youth, in particular, the development of individualized instructional methods and materials must be high on the educational agenda.

Teacher Expectancies
for Student Success

In an edited volume entitled *Making Schools Work for Underachieving Minority Students* (Bain & Herman, 1990), Haycock comments:

> A lot of people interpret the title of this part of the book—
> "Promising Practices: Developing Effective Instructional
> Programs"—as suggesting that minority youngsters need
> something quite different from other youngsters. The notion
> here somehow is we educate all kids the same. But
> somehow, Black kids, Brown kids, and poor kids don't
> learn as much. That is a serious misconception. In fact,
> we do not educate all children the same way. Into the
> education of minority and poor youngsters we put less

of everything that we believe makes a difference in terms of quality education. We put in less instructional time. We put less in the way of well-trained teachers; less in the way of rigorous higher order curriculum; less in the way of interesting books. Perhaps most important of all, we put in less in the way of teachers who believe students can learn. (p. 53)

Ann and Russ, two fictional upper elementary reading specialists, and also good friends, meet at their school the week before the fall term begins. We catch them in conversation:

> Ann: When I was in the office, getting my own list, I saw the list of kids they've assigned to you this term.

> Russ: Yeah, I was going to pick it up this morning, but did I see a funny look on your face as you mentioned my list?

> Ann: Well, sort of. I mean I know most of the kids you've got, and they'll be OK to work with, but . . . bad news . . . you've got Billy Jones, and all I can say is good luck! I had his brother Bobby last year, and I worked so hard to get him closer to level, but he's still 2 full years behind. I swear, it must be that family's gene pool. My advice? Don't kill yourself with Billy. There's only so much of you to go around, and you might as well spend your energy where it's going to do some good.

Whether the structuring of teacher expectancy for student failure derives from assumptions about the "gene pool," as in this example, or from prevailing stereotypes in the United States about the modest potential of minority and low-income youth, a wealth of relevant research has demonstrated that teacher expectancies are significantly associated with student performance and that the nature of the association is often directional: Expectancies influence performance. In the example, when Billy Jones in fact shows poor progress in his reading skills, we are safe in assuming that one causative factor is that so little was expected of him. That circumstance, particularly for gang-attracted and gang-affiliated youth, is the bad news. However, expectational influences have also been clearly shown to operate for the better (Ashton & Webb, 1986; Brophy, 1983; Dusek, 1985; Rosenthal & Jacobson, 1968). While certainly not the sole determinant of competent academic performance, teacher expectations for student success do in fact help bring about such educational outcomes. No doubt it is easier to say than do, but it is still worthwhile to suggest: "Expect the best of your students—you may indeed get it."

With collaboration in program planning, individualization of instruction, and high teacher expectancies for student success, the stage for enrichment is set. For positive school program outcomes actually to take place, both of the main actors, teacher and student, must bring to the stage certain potentiating, success-enhancing qualities. For the teacher, the critical factor concerns the characteristics that combine to make a successful mentor. For the student, what is most important is a sufficiently high level of motivation to participate in and benefit from the planned program. It is to these two program enrichment factors—mentoring and motivation—that we now turn.

Mentoring

Several years ago a new and, to many, a rather surprising series of research findings began to emerge in a topic area that has come to be called *resiliency*. Ellis and Lane (1978); Kaufman, Grunebaum,

Cohler, and Gamer (1979); and Werner and Smith (1982) each found something unexpected in the types of poverty-stricken, crime-ridden, disorganized, problem-filled environments that had long been seen as breeding grounds for delinquency, gang-banging, and all manner of difficulties in socialization and development: a number of youths who were turning out just great! They stayed in school and did well, had friends, stayed out of trouble with the law, and, more generally, lived positive lives very different from what had been predicted and so frequently actually seen in other youths growing up in the same social and economic conditions. These adolescents were variously labeled resilient or invulnerable, or as superkids. Was there anything, investigators asked, common in the backgrounds of such youngsters that might differentiate them from other youths whose predicted bad ends came true? High on the short list of differentiating qualities was the fact that at some point during the past decade or so of their lives such youngsters had developed a strong and sustained positive relationship with an adult figure. The adult serving as mentor could be almost anyone, by role or profession— uncle, coach, cousin, priest, neighbor, parent, employer, and, not infrequently, teacher.

Given the press of diverse role demands, it is no wonder teachers often feel they have insufficient opportunity to contribute significantly to the lives of their students. Yet the resiliency studies just cited suggest that, at least in some instances, the teacher-student relationship may be the single most potent influence in a youngster's life.

It is not easy to be an enriching mentor. The task demands are wide and deep. Good mentors are available and consistent; they provide support, encouragement, connection to resources, and the wisdom of experience; they are fun to be with; and, whether formally teachers or not, they also instruct. Some of the instruction via mentorship may be actual didactic teaching, but we believe the bulk of effective mentorship comes by modeling. Youth imitate what a respected adult actually does much more than what he or she simply tells them to do. When the mentor is a classroom teacher, modeling is a day-long affair:

> Modeling effects can occur at any time, not just at those times when the teacher is deliberately trying to serve as a model. Remember, all that is required is that the students see the behavior modeled before them. . . . Teachers are responsible for living up to their own ideals, and they must remain aware of their roles as models in order to insure that most of what the students learn from observing them is positive and desirable. (Good & Brophy, 1987, p. 175)

Modeling is particularly effective when the teacher-mentor makes the effort, when appropriate, to think aloud and share with his or her students the process underlying the overt behaviors the student is observing. In this manner, students may learn curiosity, interest in learning, logical thinking, problem-solving strategies, general rules, definitions, beliefs about particular subject matter, the subject matter itself, values, attitudes, behavioral standards, respect for oneself and others, and much, much more.

We do not wish to overestimate the potential value of mentoring. Evidence to date generally suggests it may hold lesser value for youth already seriously involved in delinquent behavior. For youngsters on their way to such a pattern but not yet there (i.e., gang-attracted rather than gang-affiliated), the potential for modeling effects seems greater.

In addition to their direct purposes, active teacher mentoring— as well as collaborative program development, individualized instruction, and teacher success expectancies—may serve as sources of heightened student motivation to attend school, participate in its academic and nonacademic offerings, and derive benefit. Much the same indirect motivational enhancement may occur following student participation in the skills development programs discussed later in this chapter. But we deal in this book with students who may be especially low in such motivation. To them, school is, as noted earlier, boring, irrelevant, a waste of time, and just plain unpleasant. To motivate meaningful participation, more than indirect effects must be involved.

Student Motivation

A great deal of theory and research on motivation and its facilitation points toward student success expectations as a primary source (Bandura, 1982; Dweck & Elliott, 1985; Good & Brophy, 1987; Weiner, 1984). Anticipation of success in school, and hence motivation to strive for it, has been shown to be enhanced by the following:

◁ Giving patient encouragement, aiding the student to take intellectual risks with little fear of criticism or embarrassment and a minimum of performance anxiety

◁ Offering an appropriate level of challenge or difficulty, neither too easy nor too hard

◁ Using meaningful learning objectives—that is, material that in the student's eyes is worthwhile either in its own right or as a stepping stone to higher order objectives

◁ Helping students regularly perceive a substantial relationship between the level of effort they invest in a task and the level of task mastery they can appropriately anticipate

◁ Fostering an internal locus of control (i.e., that they and not such external causes as chance, luck, or fate largely control the outcomes of their school efforts)

◁ Offering curricular material first at the student's current level, then progressing in small, mastery-assuring steps

◁ Helping students set realistic goals and fostering commitment in trying to reach them. Good and Brophy (1987) note in this latter regard:

> Goal setting is especially effective when the goals are (1) *proximal* rather than distal (they refer to performance on a task to be attempted here and now rather than to attainment of some ultimate goal in the distant future), (2) *specific* (complete a page of math problems with no more than one error) rather than global (do a good job), and (3) *challenging* (difficult but reachable) rather than too easy or too hard. (p. 313)

◁ Providing regular, clear feedback helping the student assess his or her progress toward established goals

◁ Making abstract material personal, concrete, or familiar—by use of anecdotes, objects, demonstrations, and analogies

◁ Offering rewards as incentives for good performance—points, checks, stars, stickers, activities, privileges, recognition, and so forth

◁ Calling attention to the instrumental value of academic activities in helping students meet their current and future needs and aspirations

Even with enhanced motivation for school success and active mentoring, satisfactory student achievement will remain elusive unless the youngster has developed a repertoire of study and social skills requisite for competent functioning in school and community settings.

Study Skills

A teenager may be highly knowledgeable about automobiles and their functioning. He may know brands, models, motors, and more. Adults in his life may be willing to mentor his learning to drive, and he may be highly motivated to do so. But he will not cause the car to move (at least safely) until somehow he acquires the actual skills that constitute competent driving. He must learn the skills of the road. Study skills are the skills of the road for competent in-school functioning. As Wise, Genshaft, and Byrley (1987) note, "Study skills have been called part of an invisible curriculum because students are expected to acquire these skills and yet rarely are taught them systematically. Study skills may be one of the most neglected areas in the curriculum" (p. 67).

Several different skills are requisite:

△ Environmental management (i.e., establishing surroundings most favorable to studying—minimal distractions, necessary materials, adequate time)

△ Time management (i.e., allocation, scheduling, priorities, use of "hidden" time, identifying optimal study times, self-monitoring of time spent on task)

△ Stress management (i.e., learning to relax, managing performance anxiety, self-talk, goal setting)

△ Concentration (i.e., reducing internal and external distractions, underlining, time on task, making outlines, defining terms, rereading, taking breaks)

△ Forgetting and remembering (i.e., organizing information meaningfully, learning selectively, reinforcing new ideas by association, rehearsing through recitation, using short study periods, concept mapping)

◁ Reading and listening (i.e., raising useful questions, outlining, mastering note taking, dictionary skills, improving reading speed and comprehension, summarizing)

◁ Managing test anxiety (i.e., starting early, staying on top of course work, organizing material, cramming systematically, time-use strategies)

Social Skills

In addition to their central and traditional mandate to impart basic cognitive skills and knowledge to students, schools have increasingly become the vehicle for teaching a wide array of social skills. Perhaps school-based efforts to instill and enhance the interpersonal, conflict management, anger control, and people-skill competencies of children and adolescents have taken root so rapidly and firmly because the older, more traditional arenas in which they are imparted—home, church, mass media—have recently performed much less well in doing so.

Our own social skills program, Skillstreaming, is currently in place in hundreds of schools and delinquency centers in the United States (Goldstein & McGinnis, 1997). In this approach, small groups of often chronically aggressive or delinquent adolescents are (a) shown several examples of expert use of the behaviors that constitute the skills in which they are deficient (i.e., modeling); (b) given several guided opportunities to practice and rehearse these competent behaviors (i.e., role-playing); (c) provided with praise, reinstruction, and related feedback on how well their role-playing skill enactments matched the expert model's portrayals (i.e., performance feedback); and (d) encouraged to engage in a series of activities designed to increase the chances that skills learned in the training setting will endure and be available for use when needed in school, home, community, institution, or other real-world settings (i.e., transfer training). By these means—modeling, role-playing, performance feedback, and transfer training—instruction is offered in a curriculum of 50 prosocial skills. The skills taught in this manner are listed in Table 8.

Several dozen studies of the real-world effectiveness of Skill-streaming reveal that, as others have found for all other social skills training programs, it yields high levels of skill learning but more modest levels of skill performance in school, street, home, and other settings in which youngsters operate. Our response to such unreliable generalization of skill competency was to formulate a new and potentially more potent social skills training program, Aggression Replacement Training (ART), consisting of separate weekly sessions of Skillstreaming (the *behavioral* component of ART), Anger Control Training (the *emotional* component), and Moral Reasoning Training (the *values* component; Goldstein et al., 1998). ART has been shown in a dozen efficacy evaluation studies conducted in school, community, and delinquency center settings to substantially increase social skill level and substantially reduce both aggressive incidents and the rate of criminal recidivism. Most relevant to the concerns of the present book, these felicitous outcome findings also emerged in a study evaluating ART program effectiveness with 12 highly criminal youth gangs, a study reported in our monograph "The Prosocial Gang" (Goldstein et al., 1994). Results indicated that social skills were learned, work performance improved, and, perhaps most significant, criminal recidivism was reduced. Arrest data were available for the participating youths and their respective control group. Five of the 38 ART participants (13%) and 14 of the 27 control group members (52%) were rearrested during the 8-month tracking period (Chi square = 6.08, p<.01). We consider such findings to be a strong affirmation of the utility of social skills training for gang-involved youth.

Table 8—The Skillstreaming Curriculum for Adolescents

Group I: Beginning Social Skills
1. Listening
2. Starting a Conversation
3. Having a Conversation
4. Asking a Question
5. Saying Thank You
6. Introducing Yourself
7. Introducing Other People
8. Giving a Compliment

Group II: Advanced Social Skills
9. Asking for Help
10. Joining In
11. Giving Instructions
12. Following Instructions
13. Apologizing
14. Convincing Others

Group III: Skills for Dealing with Feelings
15. Knowing Your Feelings
16. Expressing Your Feelings
17. Understanding the Feelings of Others
18. Dealing with Someone Else's Anger
19. Expressing Affection
20. Dealing with Fear
21. Rewarding Yourself

Group IV: Skill Alternatives to Aggression
22. Asking Permission
23. Sharing Something

Note. From *Skillstreaming the Adolescent: New Strategies and Perspectives for Teaching Prosocial Skills* (rev. ed., pp. 66–67) by A.P. Goldstein and E. McGinnis, 1997, Champaign, IL: Research Press. Reprinted by permission.

Table 8—The Skillstreaming Curriculum for Adolescents CONTINUED

24. Helping Others
25. Negotiating
26. Using Self-Control
27. Standing Up for Your Rights
28. Responding to Teasing
29. Avoiding Trouble with Others
30. Keeping Out of Fights

Group V: Skills for Dealing with Stress

31. Making a Complaint
32. Answering a Complaint
33. Being a Good Sport
34. Dealing with Embarrassment
35. Dealing with Being Left Out
36. Standing Up for a Friend
37. Responding to Persuasion
38. Responding to Failure
39. Dealing with Contradictory Messages
40. Dealing with an Accusation
41. Getting Ready for a Difficult Conversation
42. Dealing with Group Pressure

Group VI: Planning Skills

43. Deciding on Something to Do
44. Deciding What Caused a Problem
45. Setting a Goal
46. Deciding on Your Abilities
47. Gathering Information
48. Arranging Problems by Importance
49. Making a Decision
50. Concentrating on a Task

In addition to study and social skills training, in-school programming for gang-attracted and gang-affiliated youth may be enriched by involving fellow students as collaborators in the teaching-learning enterprise. Two well-established pedagogical means for doing so are cooperative learning and peer and cross-age tutoring.

Cooperative Learning

Cooperative learning is both a philosophy of teaching and a series of several different but related teaching methods. Across areas of academic content, most of these methods involve a heterogeneous group of youngsters working together on a shared task or project (e.g., a cooperative task structure) and the provision of grades or other rewards to the group as a whole based upon either the sum of individual improvement scores or the group's overall task performance (e.g., a cooperative incentive structure). Contemporary cooperative learning approaches seek to express principles of cooperative incentive and task structures; task specialization; distributed or shared group leadership; heterogeneous group membership; positive interdependence among this membership; individual accountability; high levels of group autonomy; equal opportunity scoring based on improvement compared to self, not others; and between-group, not within-group, competition. The following approaches to cooperative learning illustrate these various principles.

Student Teams–Achievement Divisions. In Slavin's (1978) Student Teams–Achievement Divisions (STAD), four- or five-member learning teams are constituted. Ideally, youngsters assigned to each team represent the heterogeneity of the larger class, school, or community (i.e., boys and girls; high-, average-, and low-performing students; students of different ethnic or racial backgrounds). The teacher regularly introduces new learning materials. In a peer-tutoring format, students study the materials together, take turns quizzing one another, discuss the materials as a group, or use other self-selected means to master the material.

193

The teacher communicates to each team that study of any given material is not complete until all teammates are sure they understand it. The teacher transforms quiz scores into team scores, with each student's contribution to the team score being not the absolute level of performance but, instead, the amount of improvement in that student's score over his or her past average score.

Teams-Games-Tournaments. The Teams-Games-Tournaments (TGT) approach to cooperative learning, developed by DeVries and Slavin (1978), employs the same team structure, instructional format, and worksheets as STAD. Instead of quizzes, however, students engage in cross-team academic games as the means for demonstrating their individual mastery of the subject matter. These games are played in weekly tournaments in which students compete against other teams, comparable in past performance.

Team Assisted Individualization. Team Assisted Individualization (TAI) was developed by Slavin, Leavey, and Madden (1982) for use when the members of a class are too heterogeneous to be taught the same material at the same rate. TAI has been used primarily for the cooperative learning of mathematics. The student works at his or her own pace—reading instructions, working on successive skill sheets, taking "checkouts," and being tested. This progression occurs in self-selected teams of two students each. Team members exchange answer sheets and check each other's skill sheets and checkouts.

Jigsaw. In Jigsaw, students are assigned to heterogeneous six-member teams, and the academic material to be covered is broken down into sections. For example, Aronson, Blaney, Stephan, Sikes, and Snapp (1978) describe a fifth-grade Jigsaw classroom in which biographies of great Americans were being studied. The teacher created five biographies that respectively described the famous figures' ancestors and arrival in the United States; childhood and adolescence; early adulthood, education, and employment; middle years and their highlights; and events in society at large during this latter period. Each team member was assigned one of these sections to read and study in order to become expert (six team members for five sections were used to cover absentees). Members of different teams who had studied the same sections then met as "expert groups" to consider their sections. Having thus become experts by study and discussion, students then returned to their own teams and took turns teaching their teammates about their sections.

Jigsaw II. Unlike Jigsaw, in which team members are responsible for a unique section of the material, Jigsaw II requires all students to read the same chapter or story. Each student is, however, assigned a topic within this context in which to become expert. As in Jigsaw, the students from each group assigned the same topic meet in expert groups to discuss the topic and then return to their own teams to teach what they have learned. Individual quizzes are taken, and scores for individual improvement over previous performances are computed and used as the basis for determining an overall team score.

Learning Together. Learning Together (Johnson & Johnson, 1975) is the most group-oriented of the cooperative learning alternatives. Students work on assignment sheets in heterogeneous four- or five-member groups. The group members hand in for evaluation a single assignment sheet from all of them. As the method's title indicates, they then receive feedback as a group regarding how well they are "learning together." Reflecting a cooperative incentive structure, grades are based on the average achievement scores of individual members.

Group Investigation. Cooperative learning via the Group Investigation method (Sharon & Sharon, 1976) is a six-stage process initiated and conducted by the participating students themselves. It involves the following steps:

1. Identifying the topic and organizing into self-selected two- to six-member groups

2. Planning the learning task, in which the members choose subtopics for investigation

3. Carrying out the investigation

4. Preparing a final report

5. Presenting the final report, as a group, to the class as a whole

6. Evaluating themselves in collaboration with the teacher

These seven approaches to cooperative learning are the more frequently utilized and more thoroughly evaluated of those in existence. The typical classroom in this country, however, is far less cooperative. Rather than working together for group rewards (i.e., cooperative task and incentive structures), most classes are organized according to an individualistic task structure (e.g., students work alone) or a competitive incentive structure (e.g., marks assigned on a curve).

The interpersonal consequences of the cooperative, competitive, and individualistic orientations can be dramatically different. The typical classroom structure involving individualistic work for competitive rewards may be particularly damaging for low-performing youth. Slavin (1985) comments in this regard that

> for many low-performing students, no amount of effort is likely to put them at the top of the class because they have already missed so much in past years. Thus, the competition for top score in the classroom is poorly matched. Because they have such a small chance of success, low performers may give up or try to disrupt the activity. They can hardly be expected to do otherwise. ... Low performing students ... may turn to delinquency or withdrawal as a means of maintaining self-esteem in the face of what they perceive as a hostile school environment. (p. 6)

A portion of low-performing students are also members of minority groups, and a number of studies demonstrate that African American and Hispanic/Latino students appear to respond particularly well to cooperative learning experiences, perhaps because of compatible cultural group-oriented experiences (Beady & Slavin, 1981; Lucker, Rosenfield, Sikes, & Aronson, 1976; Slavin, 1977; Slavin & Oickle, 1981).

Relevant research evidence is clear, substantial, and almost uniformly positive that participation in cooperative learning programs enhances subsequent cooperative behavior. Apparently, it also does much more. Such participation has been demonstrated to increase a host of other prosocial and cognitive characteristics, including interpersonal attraction among students, internal locus of control, motivation on academic tasks, time on task, self-esteem, quality of cross-ethnic interactions, quality of cross-handicapped interaction, quality of student-teacher interaction, attitudes toward heterogeneity of peers, peer norms supporting academic performance, and, in an especially large number of investigations, academic achievement. Cooperative learning is indeed an enriching approach to schooling.

Peer and Cross-Age Tutoring

Peer and cross-age tutoring programs, like cooperative learning, make use of reciprocal interaction among students as the means of academic instruction. Unlike cooperative learning, tutoring interventions most typically involve only two students at a time, one serving as instructor (tutor), the other as learner (tutee). Peer tutoring takes place between two students of the same age; cross-age tutoring pairs an older student as tutor with a younger one as tutee. A substantial number of efficacy evaluations show such tutoring to yield impressive academic gains, as well as positive social effects (Cohen, Kulik, & Kulik, 1982; Scruggs, Mastropieri, & Richter, 1985).

Which peer-influenced intervention should be employed, if any, will depend on matters of school climate, teacher acceptance, and curricular content. As Miller and Peterson (1987) comment, for example, "Highly structured academic tasks involving considerable drill and practice . . . readily lend themselves to peer tutoring formats, while more complex tasks that involve higher-order cognitive skills may be better suited for cooperative learning programs" (p. 89).

Such considerations are important, as are the delivery parameters of any curricular approach. We wish to emphasize here, however, the likely enrichment consequences of peer-mediated educational programming for youths having difficulty in school, playing out marginalized roles, finding their school days to be more like "school daze," and thus inclining toward serious gang involvement.

While in this chapter we have highlighted a broad array of means for in-school enrichment programming for gang-attracted and gang-affiliated youth, we most certainly have not exhausted the possibilities. Other options include vocational education, job and career awareness sessions, increased extracurricular recreational and social opportunities, health screening and treatment services, child care services, and legal aid. These and other offerings are increasingly coming to constitute what Dryfoos (1994) has described as the "full-service school." Each of these enrichment services may serve the central goals of increasing relevance, decreasing boredom, and, in general, more fully connecting at-risk youth to a rewarding schooling process.

COMMUNITY-BASED ENRICHMENT PROGRAMMING

The recent and rapid spread of gangs across the United States to urban, suburban, and rural areas has been countered by an equally dramatic increase in the number and variety of community-based attempts to moderate this expansion. Many of these attempts are police-driven and suppression-oriented, and therefore not the focus of the present volume. Perhaps several hundred other options have enrichment as their goal, and thus are our concern here.

In chapter 6, we examined a number of program qualities associated with positive program outcomes. In the remainder of this chapter, we use these facilitative program qualities as a template to select, evaluate, and recommend a number of community-based gang prevention and intervention programs currently or recently operating in the United States. What follows is not a directory of services, but rather a series of examples of community-based gang enrichment programs worth emulating. We have chosen these examples from the many dozens available because they possess the qualities we have identified as characteristic of effective community-based programming.

Each is, first of all, *prosocial.* Enrichment, enhancement, and expansion are its overarching goals, not merely suppression. Each is *comprehensive* in its offerings. The domains of need and reme-diation for gang-attracted and gang-affiliated youth are numerous and diverse. Program content must be comprehensive to meet such needs. The offerings thus provided must be *coordinated;* the separate components of the program must fit together and complement and build upon one another. A gang prevention/intervention effort must also be sustained—that is, it must possess *program intensity.* A week climbing ropes in the woods or sailing in the ocean or on a wagon train in the desert may be interesting and enjoyable but is hardly up to changing years of the types of antisocial learning that gang or near-gang involvement yields. Thus, to be worth exploring, programs must possess both the breadth (i.e., comprehensiveness) and depth (i.e., duration) that constitute program intensity. Finally, program effectiveness must be *evaluated.* Far too many community-based programs begin and continue based upon impression, anec-dote, or no evidence at all. Those next described, with few exceptions, have been carefully and independently evaluated for their real-world impact on participating youth.

Boys and Girls Clubs of America

Boys and Girls Clubs of America has 1,450 clubs nationwide. One representative club prevention effort, operated primarily from a location in an inner-city housing development, is being implemented in a medium-sized Midwestern city. The area has organized gang activity. The main prevention activity is after-school programming. Young people participate in a tutoring/homework assistance session, which is followed by organized sports, field trips, group discussions (on relevant topics, such as substance abuse), and other activities. A primary goal is to keep these youths involved beyond the project time period and to retain them as club members. Programming continues through the summer months, with various planned activities offered as alternatives to the streets.

A representative consortium effort is being implemented in a large city in the Northeast. The designated club is located amidst several housing developments with organized gang activity and generally very poor conditions. Beyond providing after-school activities of the sort just described, the club also works intensively to involve other community organizations in a network associated with its efforts, as well as to involve parents on a regular basis (e.g., in regular discussion sessions built around an evening meal). The network includes direct links with a local middle school, with housing authority police and other local law enforcement personnel, and with other organizations. In addition, this effort has focused on providing recreational and educational activities that expose participants to experiences beyond the inner city. Field trips, overnight campouts, and other excursions are intended to take participants literally beyond the limits of the neighborhoods or housing areas where they spend most of their time. Club staff work to make the facility a safe and neutral place, sheltered from the dangers of the surrounding area.

Another Boys and Girls Clubs intervention effort is situated in a large Western city, in an area with extensive gang activity. Targeting older youths, this effort involves after-school activities, including tutorials and various recreational opportunities. Much attention is devoted to organizing and conducting sports-related outings and educational trips, such as museum visits and the like. Part of the club effort entails transporting gang-involved youths to a camp setting, where local deputy sheriffs participate in the camp activities. The purpose of this experience is to provide positive individual contact and attention and, ultimately, to promote changes in attitude. Club staff also visit probation detention facilities, where they help incarcerated youths maintain contact with family and friends and facilitate visits. Staff assist the young people in planning for their return to the community, searching for employment, and dealing with other issues. The aim is twofold: to advocate for youths and to convey a message of community concern.

Getting Out

Getting Out is a program developed by the Boys and Girls Clubs of St. Paul, Minnesota (1997). It was developed in partnership with the St. Paul Police, Ramsey County Juvenile Probation, United Methodist Hospital, Dr. James Foley, and the Ramsey County Youth Gang Task Force. Located adjacent to a public housing development occupied by a large percentage of new Southeast Asian immigrant families, the program serves youths of all ethnic backgrounds. Boys and Girls Clubs programs emphasize supervised, community-based recreational activities, which are evaluated as promising by the Office of Justice Programs' review of programs (Sherman et al., 1997). Beyond this, additional attributes of the program include a strong community partnership, location in the neighborhood served, accessibility to all residents, and comprehensive, inclusive social service programming.

What is unique about this program is the addition of a behavior-contingent gang tattoo removal program. Up to 25 former gang members can be served at one time. Candidates are gang members who express a desire to leave the gang, who are under 19 years of age, and who may or may not have gang tattoos. Those who have tattoos have them removed in stages through laser treatment. Removal sessions are spaced evenly over the course of a year, during which time the participant must complete comprehensive treatment involving education, community service, life skills training, supervised recreation, and job counseling, among other requirements. For each month in the program, participants must perform 10 hours of community service. Removal of stigmatizing gang tattoos allows participants to distance themselves more easily from the gang and from permanent recognition in the community as former gang members. While the effect of tattoo removal has not yet been evaluated, we find this aspect of the program promising.

Youth Build

Under the auspices of the National Youth Build Coalition of New York City, Boston, Cleveland, St. Louis, and San Francisco, Youth Build programs are for out-of-school low-income youths ages 16 to 23 who need employment training and education. Time in the program is evenly divided between work and education: One week participants work at a construction site, and the next they are based at the agency for educational and youth development activities. The education program emphasizes development of cognitive skills and the application of those skills to the work site. Participants learn construction skills in on-the-job training under the direct supervision of a skilled site supervisor and in the classroom. The youths work in small crews on building renovation projects in their own community; the buildings are abandoned city-owned properties. Once a building is completed, it is designated for homeless and low-income tenants and is owned and managed by a local nonprofit organization. The program stresses leadership training; it involves youths in program governance through participation in the program's policy committee, a body responsible for staffing, program policy, budget, and community action.

Participants receive regular individual and group counseling, as well as career counseling, initial job placement, and 6 months of job placement follow-up services. Youths are encouraged to continue to use job placement services as needed and for as long as needed after they leave the program. Youths also participate in peer counseling and complete an intensive 2-week leadership development program. Trainees not drawn to construction as a career are encouraged to complete the program but at any point along the way can get assistance in finding jobs related to their career goals.

Golden Eagles

Golden Eagles is a community center–based program for Native American youth living in the Phillips Community of Minneapolis, Minnesota. The program has been extensively evaluated and incorporates much of the best of what is known about community youth crime prevention. Located in the Minneapolis American Indian Center, the program serves nearly 500 youth in a single year. School-age youth may arrive at the center on foot or by private car but are commonly picked up at school at the end of the day and transported to supervised, constructive after-school activities. Academic tutoring is provided, as is skill building in conventional and traditional Native American arts and crafts. Life skills development is addressed through instruction in refusal skills, healthy life-styles, nutrition, personal safety skills, cultural roles, and traditional Native American values. Interacting with conventional Native American role models, participating in community service projects, gaining access to expanded community activities, and having a safe place are strong attributes of Golden Eagles. While self-selection by youth and families may affect outcomes somewhat, evidence indicates that Golden Eagles participants do far better on community and school measures of behavior, drug and alcohol use, and violent behavior than do matched nonparticipants (Golden Eagles Program, 1997).

Big Brothers/Big Sisters of America

Big Brothers/Big Sisters of America is a federation of agencies serving primarily at-risk adolescents and children by providing mentoring services through a professionally supported one-to-one relationship with a caring adult. Mentors must make a substantial time commitment, meeting with youth regularly for at least a year. Via a wide variety of shared activities—shopping, sports, going to the movies, discussing schoolwork, watching television—a relationship builds, ideas about life and living are exchanged, values are communicated, and skills are taught.

Evaluations examining the impact of such programming on mentored youth reveal improved family and peer relations, substantially less substance use and abuse, better school performance, and significantly less use of aggressive behavior to settle disputes (Feyerherm, Pope, & Lovell, 1992).

Gang Peace/First

The services that Gang Peace/First of Roxbury, Massachusetts, provides are health education, neighborhood outreach and youth advocacy, staff-facilitated peer counseling, tutoring, job finding, and recreational activities. Outreach workers recruit members from the streets and through public relations efforts conducted in the schools and other public forums.

Counselor-advocates provide referrals and follow up on those referrals. Gang Peace/First networks with agencies providing substance abuse counseling, housing, health care, job training, and education. Because the program maintains regular contact with participants, staff are able to continue working with those who are having difficulties at work or have been fired from employment. Gang Peace/First works through its resource network to develop jobs with area employers, and it maintains a placement database to assist neighborhood youths in the job search. A resource database on starting small businesses has been developed to help young people learn about entrepreneurship. The program also conducts educational workshops on ways to get a job and keep it; politics and political participation; community subculture; drugs, violence, and AIDS; youth and drugs; and youth, the American dream, and entrepreneurship. Gang Peace/First gives young people a place to be and an opportunity to learn about choices. The program makes a commitment to those it serves for as long as the youths feel the need of services. The features of the model—a grassroots, community base; involvement of youths in program development and operations; a long-term commitment to providing members with needed services; an individualized approach to members; cultural sensitivity; and service flexibility based on a well-developed resource network—can be replicated.

New Jersey's School-Based Youth Services Program

New Jersey's youth services program began in the mid-1980s as a coordinated program run through community centers in the high schools. It uses school buildings as activity centers in the afternoons and evenings. The New Jersey program seeks to increase recreation and activity services in after-school hours, on weekends, and during summer vacation months, as well as to provide linkages to health and other human services.

The program's overall purpose is to provide the adolescent population, especially high-risk youths, with the opportunity to complete their education, to obtain skills that lead to employment or further education, and to lead physically and mentally healthy, drug-free lives.

Each site offers a comprehensive "core package" of services, including the following:

◁ Employment counseling, training, and placement

◁ Summer and part-time job development

◁ Drug and alcohol abuse counseling

◁ Academic counseling

◁ Primary and preventive health services

◁ Recreation

◁ Referrals to health and social services

The Neutral Zone

The Neutral Zone, located in Mountainlake Terrace, Washington, was envisioned as a site at which at-risk youth might safely congregate voluntarily during the times and days of the week coinciding with high rates of criminal activity in most communities—weekend hours between 10:00 P.M. and 2:00 A.M. It was located in a local elementary school and offered a variety of services designed to be both useful and attractive to community youth. Included were recreational and social opportunities (e.g., basketball, music, movies, free food), individual counseling, job skills training, and several educational programs.

The effectiveness of Neutral Zone participation was systematically evaluated by means of direct observation of participating youth, focus group interviews with participants, and police department crime data for the months covered by the evaluation. All three sources of evaluation data indicated positive program effects not only for actual time in program, but also during post-program periods (Thurman, Giacomazzi, Reisig, & Mueller, 1996).

Youth Works

Located in Louisville, Kentucky, Youth Works is a juvenile court diversion program whose main intervention mode is mentoring. Mentor-youth meetings may be frequent but are weekly at minimum. Services provided by these means may be educational, recreational, counseling, brokering, and more. The program's literature states, regarding the mentor's role:

Help youth explore interests. Develop a trusting relationship, provide guidance and a listening ear. Provide services
such as practicing job interviews or teaching youth to ride
a bus. Make initial home visit with youth and his/her
family. Participate in information gathering and utilization
of community resources. Identify youth's strengths and
areas for growth and work with staff in developing case
planning for youth. (Youth Works, 1997, p. 4)

El Puente

El Puente (the Bridge), located in Brooklyn, New York, considers its program of services to be holistic, emphasizing the integration of recreation, education, and social service projects to enrich the minds, bodies, and spirits of its participants (Lovell & Pope, 1993). Recreational programming includes dance, drama, art, culture club, ethnic dance, athletics (e.g., basketball, boxing), and an Outward Bound program, in which youths participate in wilderness skills training and in a community service project. Educational programming involves Graduate Equivalency Degree (GED) and English as a Second Language (ESL) courses, homework assistance, counseling, the New York–based "I Have a Dream" program, and combined learning and service projects (e.g., murals on such topics as AIDS, Young Latinos for Peace). Holistic programming provides and supports the personal growth of young people. There are peer counselors, short- and long-term goals for each participant, and a medical unit to see to health needs.

The Little Village

The Little Village is a program collaboratively run by the Chicago Police Department (Neighborhood Relations Unit), community youth workers from the University of Chicago, and a community-based organization, Neighbors against Gang Violence. It consists of both a suppression component—namely, increased police and probation supervision—and a number of enrichment components. The latter include family support, job training, jobs, counseling, and other social interventions and opportunities provision. Evaluation of this program, based on pre-post report by both police and participating gang members, has revealed a substantial decrease in violent crimes committed in comparison with both preprogram level and with neighborhoods surrounding the program area (Spergel, 1996).

Project SAY

Project SAY (Save-A-Youth) is a collaborative effort of the Anaheim, California, YMCA, Boys and Girls Club, Salvation Army, Parks and Recreation Department, and Community Service Department. Programming includes a major recreational component, individual counseling, classes for parents, a police "ride-along" program, a summer camp project, and a "street school" set up in a local community facility to offer remedial opportunities to youths who have dropped out of regular school. Evaluations of this program have been anecdotal and show a substantial number of participating youth become regular school attenders and participants—also on a regular basis—in program-sponsored recreational activities.

The Comin' Up Program

This multiservice program in Fort Worth, Texas, is provided by school, police, probation, parks and recreation, and religious organizations. It is targeted particularly to gang youth and their families, offering academic, conflict resolution, peer mediation, and job and communication skills training. An unusual aspect of this program, related to its placement at several different community locations, is its employment of intersite activities. Ranging from dances to sports to community service activities, these events provide opportunities for participating youth to practice skills, participate cooperatively, and meet and learn about youth from different parts of the program city and their different cultural worlds.

Academy High School

Designed for at-risk, acting-out youth with a history of challenging authority and poor school attendance, Academy High School in Paterson, New Jersey, is an alternative, nontraditional secondary school, physically located at and part of a community college campus. While involving its own teaching personnel, the school utilizes regular college classrooms and facilities (gymnasium, lounges, etc.). Classes are small, the student-teacher ratio is low (5 to 1), expectations and standards for performance are clear, and counseling and similar services are available.

Results of participation have included high levels of attendance and graduation, as well as clearly improved in-class performance. As one report evaluating this innovative program observed:

> The theory from the beginning was to place the program
> on a college campus in order to positively influence
> students through their participation in the college setting
> and in the wider college community. This theory has
> proven to be well-founded. The freedom and flexibility
> offered by the college environment as well as the daily
> contact with college students, staff and faculty have been
> extremely positive. (Shereskewsky & Ross, 1997, p. 26)

Project BUILD

Project Broader Urban Involvement and Leadership Development (BUILD) is a Chicago-based prevention program consisting of a gang prevention curriculum and an after-school program. The curriculum, oriented toward middle-school adolescents, focuses on the nature of gangs, gang violence, substance abuse in gangs, gang recruitment, consequences of membership, and more. Following completion of the curriculum, youths seen as at risk for gang membership are invited to participate in BUILD's after-school program, a program comprehensively providing recreational activities, job skills training, educational assistance, and social activities. BUILD's curricular and after-school program has been shown, at least on a short-term basis, to positively influence the likelihood that an at-risk youth will avoid gang membership (Thompson & Jason, 1988).

Project RAISE

Located in Baltimore, Maryland, Project RAISE is a mentoring program for at-risk youth. Participating youngsters are typically provided with a mentor on a long-term basis, starting in sixth grade (or earlier) and continuing until high school graduation. Mentoring over this several year span provides participating youth a trusting, dependable relationship; nonjudgmental listening; an introduction to vocational, social, recreational, and other community opportunities; and, especially in the case of this project, heightened attachment to school participation and improved school performance. Independent evaluation of this program has in fact demonstrated both decreased school dropout and improved academic achievement (McPartland & Nettles, 1993).

Communities in Schools

Headquartered in Alexandria, Virginia, and implemented in dozens of sites in the U.S., Communities in Schools (CIS), in both its in-school classroom version and its community-site alternative school model, assigns each youth at high risk for school dropout a case manager to provide or broker a wide range of relevant services. These include directly school-relevant services (e.g., tutoring, remedial education), legal services, counseling, job-finding and job-keeping skills training, and more.

As noted in the *Juvenile Justice Bulletin:*

A student's "decision" to drop out of school might be the product of many factors, including family problems, drug and alcohol abuse, illiteracy, and teenage pregnancy. Therefore, the entire community, not just the schools, must take responsibility for preventing youth from dropping out of school. CIS brings together businesses and public and private agencies in communities—welfare and health professionals, employment counselors, social workers and recreation leaders, the clergy, and members of community groups—and puts them where they're needed—in the schools. CIS treats the student and his or her family in a holistic manner, bringing together in one place a support system of caring adults who ensure that the student has access to the resources that can help him or her build self-worth and the skills needed to embark on a more productive and constructive life. (U.S. Office of Juvenile Justice and Delinquency Prevention, 1997, p. 1)

Communities in Schools has demonstrated that such individualized and comprehensive programming can substantially reduce the school dropout rate for at-risk youth.

Gulf Coast Trades Center

As its name implies, vocational training is the core offering of the Gulf Coast Trades Center in New Waverly, Texas, a residential center for adjudicated youth. Building trades, culinary arts, office systems, and auto technology are among the vocational skills taught. In addition, remedial education, substance abuse services, recreational programs, individual and group counseling, and job skills training are also provided. Taken together, the program goal is to "promote the social and economic independence of disadvantaged youth . . . who are adjudicated and at risk of life long dependency" (Buzbee, 1997, p. 2).

Formal tracking of follow-up outcomes reveals consistently high levels of post-release job placement and consistently low levels of reincarceration (Intercultural Development Research Association, 1988).

Collaborative Intensive Community Treatment Program

Competency development is the overriding enrichment goal of this multiagency program in Erie, Pennsylvania. The program is directed to adjudicated youth on either a diversion basis or on a post-release basis following incarceration. Agencies collaborating and coordinating their offerings include the Erie County School District, Office of Human Services, Office of Children and Youth Services, Juvenile Probation, and a multisite community treatment agency, Perseus House Alternative Treatment Program, Inc. Using school settings as program sites, the program provides, on a 7-day-a-week basis, educational services, social skills and anger management training, recreational activities, and other "wraparound" services as needed. An additional feature of this program is compulsory attendance at weekend parenting skills sessions by the youths' parents. Systematic evaluation of this program has revealed significant benefit in school attendance, school achievement, and lowered crime recidivism rates (Goldstein et al., 1998).

SUMMARY

Gang participation is often a powerful magnet for many youth. Preventing the gang-attracted youth from joining is not easily done, and even more difficult is weaning out from membership those already gang-affiliated. Such challenges require equally powerful means, and we assert that such means must go beyond control measures to include school and community enrichment offerings.

We must "sweeten the day" for at-risk youngsters by providing in both their school and nonschool lives rich opportunities to learn, develop competence and enhanced self-worth, attach themselves more fully to traditional means for achieving life satisfaction, and enjoy themselves while doing so.

CONCLUSION

A Future Perspective

The gang situation in the United States is quite likely to continue to worsen. The number of gangs and gang-affiliated youth will continue to grow substantially. This dire prediction is much more than an extrapolation from past trends. It rests on straightforward demographics. Currently, there are 25 million individuals in the U.S. ages 13 to 21. It is expected that by the year 2010, there will be 31.1 million such persons ("Juvenile Population," 1997). Thus, beyond projections from the exponential growth of ganging in past decades, our assertion is based first of all on the sheer numbers of gang-age youth.

For gang growth and its attendant aggressive behaviors actually to occur, this expanding adolescent cohort must grow up in a society that teaches, encourages, supports, and rewards the acquisition and enactment of aggression. Such is sadly an accurate depiction of our society. For gang-initiated violence to be lethal, it must occur in a societal context characterized by easy availability of lethal weaponry. There are 220 million privately owned guns in the United States today (Goldstein, 1996), a marker we believe of much that is wrong about this country and most certainly a major facilitator of youth and gang violence.

Past gang growth trends, predicted demographics, the teaching and encouragement of aggression, and the wide availability of lethal means for the expression of aggression are, perhaps, the necessary but insufficient conditions underlying our prediction of gang increases in the future. For such a prediction to become reality, there also must be a dearth of alternative outlets for youth to meet their legitimate and quite typical adolescent needs and aspirations, and to discourage their antisocial desires. Were the United States to augment—rather than diminish, as in fact it has—the social, recreational, vocational, and educational resources that permit enhanced self-esteem, the development of positive identity, peer group formation and participation, and a sense of hope for the future, perhaps a substantial number of youth would be less drawn to gang membership in the first place.

We assert that the gang situation in this country is likely to worsen. But probability is not inevitability. At least to some extent, our destiny is in our own hands. The aphorism offered by those decrying quick fixes and championing long-term solutions—"You pay now, or pay (usually more) later"—certainly applies here. Supervised, validated, and data-driven social, recreational, vocational, and educational resources must be developed and sustained in our communities.

In tandem with such progress, our schools must be prepared for what is likely to come. It is our hope that the information we have provided and the gang control and enrichment programming we have recommended are useful contributions toward such necessary preparation.

References

American School Health Association. (1989). *National Adolescent Student Health Survey.* Oakland, CA: Third Party.

Appier, J. (1990). Juvenile crime control: Los Angeles law enforcement and the Zoot Suit riots. In L. Knafla (Ed.), *Criminal justice history: An international annual* (Vol. 11). London: Meckler.

Aronson, E., Blaney, N., Stephan, C., Sikes, J., & Snapp, M. (1978). *The Jigsaw classroom.* Beverly Hills, CA: Sage.

Aronson, E., & Mills, J. (1959). The effects of severity of initiation on liking for a group. *Journal of Abnormal and Social Psychology, 59,* 177–181.

Ashton, P., & Webb, R. (1986). *Making a difference: Teachers' sense of efficacy and student achievement.* New York: Longman.

Bain, J.G., & Herman, J.L. (Eds.). (1990). *Making schools work for under-achieving minority students.* New York: Greenwood.

Bak, R. (1992, December). Dusting off the Purple Gang. *Detroit Monthly,* pp. 67–70, 109.

Bandura, A. (1982). Self-efficacy mechanism in human agency. *American Psychologist, 37,* 121–147.

Beady, C., & Slavin, R.E. (1981). Making success available to all students in desegregated schools. *Integrated Education, 18,* 28–31.

Bell, C., & Jenkins, E. (1990). Preventing black homicide. In J. Dewart (Ed.), *The state of black America.* New York: National Urban League.

Bethel School District No. 403 v. Fraser, 106 S.Ct. 3159 (1986)

Block, A. (1977). The battered teacher. *Today's Education, 66,* 58–62.

Boys and Girls Clubs of St. Paul. (1997). *Getting Out: A tattoo removal gang intervention program.* St. Paul, MN: Author.

Brophy, J.E. (1983). Research on the self-fulfilling prophecy and teacher expectations. *Journal of Educational Psychology, 75,* 631–661.

Bry, B.H. (1982). Reducing the incidence of adolescent problems through preventive intervention: One- and five-year follow up. *American Journal of Community Psychology, 10,* 265–276.

Burke, J. (1991). Teenagers, clothes, and violence. *Educational Leadership, 49,* 11–13.

Burke, N.D. (1993). Commentary: Restricting gang clothing in the public school. *Education Law Reporter, 80,* 513–526.

Buzbee, T.M. (1997). *1996 annual report.* New Waverly, TX: Gulf Coast Trades Center.

Carroll, J. (1963). A model of school learning. *Teachers College Record, 64,* 722–733.

Cartledge, G., & Johnson, C.T. (1997). School violence and cultural diversity. In A.P. Goldstein & J.C. Conoley (Eds.), *School violence intervention: A practical handbook.* New York: Guilford.

Center to Prevent Handgun Violence. (1990). *Caught in the crossfire: A report on gun violence in our nation's schools.* Washington, DC: Author.

Chin, K. (1990). Chinese gangs and extortion. In C.R. Huff (Ed.), *Gangs in America.* Newbury, CA: Sage.

Chin, K. (1996). *Chinatown gangs: Extortion, enterprise and ethnicity.* New York: Oxford University Press.

Cohen, P.A., Kulik, J.A., & Kulik, C.C. (1982). Educational outcomes of tutoring: A meta-analysis of findings. *American Educational Research Journal, 19,* 237–248.

Comstock, G. (1983). Media influences on aggression. In Center for Research on Aggression (Ed.), *Prevention and control of aggression.* New York: Pergamon.

Cox, S.M., Davidson, W.S., & Bynum, T.S. (1995). A meta-analytic assessment of delinquency-related outcomes of Alternative Education Programs. *Crime & Delinquency, 41,* 219–235.

Cronbach, L.J., & Snow, R.E. (1977). *Aptitude and instructional methods.* New York: Irvington.

Csikszentmihalyi, M., & Larsen, R. (1978). *Intrinsic rewards in school crime.* Hackensack, NJ: National Council on Crime and Delinquency.

Csikszentmihalyi, M., Larsen, R., & Prescott, S. (1977). The ecology of adolescent activities and experience. *Journal of Youth and Adolescence, 6,* 281–294.

Curry, G.D., & Spergel, I.A. (1988). Gang homicide, delinquency and community. *Criminology, 26,* 381–405.

Curry, G.D., & Spergel, I.A. (1992). Gang involvement and delinquency among Hispanic and African-American adolescent males. *Journal of Research in Crime and Delinquency, 29,* 273–292.

DeVries, D.L., & Slavin, R.E. (1978). Teams-Games-Tournaments (TGT): Review of ten classroom experiments. *Journal of Research and Development in Education, 12,* 28–38.

Dodge, K.A. (1993). Social cognitive mechanisms in the development of conduct disorder and depression. *Annual Review of Psychology, 44,* 559–584.

Donahue, T.S. (1989). *Weapons in schools* (Juvenile Justice Bulletin). Washington, DC: U.S. Department of Justice.

Dryfoos, J.G. (1994). *Full-service schools.* San Francisco: Jossey-Bass.

Dunston, L. (1990). *Reaffirming prevention: Report of the Task Force on Juvenile Gangs.* Albany: New York State Division for Youth.

Dusek, J. (1985). *Teacher expectancies.* Hillsdale, NJ: Erlbaum.

Dweck, C., & Elliott, E. (1985). Achievement motivation. In P. Mussen (Ed.), *Handbook of child psychology: Vol. 4. Socialization, personality, and social development* (4th ed.). New York: Wiley.

Ellis, R.A., & Lane, W.C. (1978). Structural supports for upward mobility. *American Sociological Review, 53,* 743–756.

Evenrud, L. (1997, February). Structuring dress code policies for safer schools. *School Safety Update* (National School Safety Center News Service), pp. 1–4.

Feyerherm, W., Pope, C., & Lovell, R. (1992). *Youth gang prevention and early intervention programs: Final research report.* Portland, OR: Boys and Girls Clubs of America.

Flamm, S., Keith, L., & Kleppel, W. (1997). *An investigation into the Latin Kings: No tolerance for gangs in the public schools* (Report to the Special Commissioner of Investigations for New York City). School District of the City of New York.

Flanagan, J., Shanner, W., Brudner, H., & Marker, R. (1973). An individualized instructional system: PLAN. In H. Talmage (Ed.), *Systems of individualized education.* Berkeley: McCutchan.

Gaustad, J. (1991). School response to gangs and violence. *Oregon School Study Council Bulletin, 34*(9).

Glaser, R., & Rosner, J. (1975). Adaptive environments for learning: Curriculum aspects. In H. Talmage (Ed.), *Systems of individualized instruction.* Berkeley: McCutchan.

Golden Eagles Program. (1997, April). *Ginew/Golden Eagles 1996 annual report: Impact of violence on Minneapolis American Indian youth.* Minneapolis American Indian Center.

Goldstein, A.P. (1971). *Psychotherapeutic attraction.* New York: Pergamon.

Goldstein, A.P. (1991). *Delinquent gangs: A psychological perspective.* Champaign, IL: Research Press.

Goldstein, A.P. (1994). Aggression toward persons and property in America's schools. *The School Psychologist, 48,* 1, 6, 18, 21.

Goldstein, A.P. (1996). *Violence in America.* Palo Alto, CA: Davies-Black.

Goldstein, A.P., & Conoley, J.C. (Eds.). (1997). *School violence intervention: A practical handbook.* New York: Guilford.

Goldstein, A.P., Glick, B., Carthan, W., & Blancero, D. (1994). *The prosocial gang.* Thousand Oaks, CA: Sage.

Goldstein, A.P., Glick, B., & Gibbs, J.C. (1998). *Aggression Replacement Training: A comprehensive intervention for aggressive youth* (rev. ed.). Champaign, IL: Research Press.

Goldstein, A.P., & Huff, C.R. (Eds.). (1993). *The gang intervention handbook.* Champaign, IL: Research Press.

Goldstein, A.P., & McGinnis, E. (1997). *Skillstreaming the adolescent: New strategies and perspectives for teaching prosocial skills* (rev. ed.). Champaign, IL: Research Press.

Goldstein, A.P., Palumbo, J., Striepling, S., & Voutsinas, A.M. (1995). *Break it up: A teacher's guide to managing student aggression.* Champaign, IL: Research Press.

Goldstein, A.P., & Stein, M. (1976). *Prescriptive psychotherapies.* New York: Pergamon.

Good, T.L., & Brophy, J.E. (1987). *Looking in classrooms.* New York: Harper & Row.

Gottfredson, G. (1987). Peer group interventions to reduce the risk of delinquent behavior: A selective review and a new evaluation. *Criminology, 25,* 671–714.

Gough, H.G. (1948). A sociological theory of psychopathy. *American Journal of Sociology, 53,* 359–366.

Hagedorn, J. (1988). *People and folks: Gangs, crime and the underclass in a rust belt city.* Chicago: Lake View.

Hare, R.D. (1970). *Psychopathy: Theory and research.* New York: Wiley.

Harrington-Lueker, D. (1992). Metal detectors: Schools turn to devices once aimed only at airport terrorists. *American School Board Journal, 179*(5), 26–27.

Haycock, K. (1990). Equity, relevance, and will. In J.G. Bain & J.L. Herman (Eds.), *Making schools work for underachieving minority students.* New York: Greenwood.

Hoffman, A.M. (1996). *Schools, violence, and society*. Westport, CT: Praeger.

Howell, J.C. (1996a). *Promising programs for youth gang violence and intervention* (Draft report to the National Youth Gang Center). Washington, DC: U.S. Office of Juvenile Justice and Delinquency Prevention.

Howell, J.C. (1996b) *Youth gangs: Homicides, drugs and guns* (Draft report to the National Youth Gang Center). Washington, DC: U.S. Office of Juvenile Justice and Delinquency Prevention.

Howell, J.C. (1996c). *Youth gangs, homicide, and drug trafficking* (Draft report to the National Youth Gang Center). Washington, DC: U.S. Office of Juvenile Justice and Delinquency Prevention.

Howell, J.C. (1996d). *Youth gangs in the United States: An overview* (Draft report to the National Youth Gang Center). Washington, DC: U.S. Office of Juvenile Justice and Delinquency Prevention.

Huesmann, L.R., & Miller, L.S. (1994). Long term effects of repeated exposure to media violence in childhood. In L.R. Huesmann (Ed.), *Aggressive behavior: Current perspectives*. New York: Plenum.

Intercultural Development Research Association. (1988). *An independent evaluation of at-risk youth pilot programs*. San Antonio: Author.

Jankowski, M.S. (1991). *Islands in the street*. Berkeley: University of California Press.

Joe, D., & Robinson, N. (1980). Chinatown's immigrant gangs, the new warrior class. *Criminology, 13*, 337–345.

Johnson, D.W., & Johnson, R.T. (1975). *Learning together and alone*. Englewood Cliffs, NJ: Prentice-Hall.

Juvenile population will grow substantially. (1997, March 13). *The New York Times*, pp. 1, 17.

Kaufman, C., Grunebaum, H., Cohler, B.J., & Gamer, E. (1979). Superkids: Competent children of psychotic mothers. *American Journal of Psychiatry, 136*, 1398–1402.

Keller, F. (1968). Good-bye teacher! *Journal of Applied Behavior Analysis, 1,* 79–88.

Kennedy, D.M., Piehl, A.M., & Braga, A.A. (1997). Youth gun violence in Boston: Gun markets, serious juvenile offenders, and a use reduction strategy. In *Proceedings of the Third Annual Conference on Youth and Crime.* St. Paul, MN: Minnesota State Bar Association, Continuing Legal Education.

Klausmeier, H., Rossmiller, R., & Saily, M. (Eds.). (1977). *Individually guided elementary education: Concepts and practices.* New York: Academic.

Klein, M.W. (1971). *Street gangs and street workers.* Englewood Cliffs, NJ: Prentice-Hall.

Klein, M.W. (1995). *The American street gang.* New York: Oxford University Press.

Klein, M.W., Maxson, C.L., & Cunningham, L.C. (1991). Crack, street gangs, and violence. *Criminology, 29,* 623–650.

Knox, G.W. (1991). *An introduction to gangs.* Barrien Springs, MI: Vande Vere.

Kodluboy, D.W. (1994). Behavioral disorders and the culture of street gangs. In R.L. Peterson & S. Ishii-Jordan, *Multicultural issues in the education of students with behavioral disorders.* Cambridge, MA: Brookline.

Kodluboy, D.W. (1996). Asian youth gangs: Basic issues for educators. *School Safety, 3,* 8–12.

Kodluboy, D.W. (1997). Gang-oriented interventions. In A.P. Goldstein & J.C. Conoley, (Eds.), *School violence intervention: A practical handbook.* New York: Guilford.

Kodluboy, D.W. (1998). [Southeast Asian youth gang study.] Unpublished data.

Kodluboy, D.W., & Evenrud, L. (1993). School-based interventions: Best practice and critical issues. In A.P. Goldstein & C.R. Huff (Eds.), *The gang intervention handbook.* Champaign, IL: Research Press.

Koklanaris, M. (1994, August 18). Area schools get set to open amid big increases in security. *Washington Times,* sec. A, p. 1.

Kounin, J. (1970). *Discipline and group management in classrooms.* New York: Holt, Rinehart & Winston.

Lemann, N. (1986a, June). The origins of the underclass. *The Atlantic Monthly,* pp. 31–55.

Lemann, N. (1986b, July). The origins of the underclass. *The Atlantic Monthly,* pp. 54–68.

Liebert, R.M., Neale, J.M., & Davidson, E.S. (1973). *The early window: Effects of television on children and youth.* New York: Pergamon.

Lipsey, M.W. (1992). Juvenile delinquency treatment: A meta-analytic inquiry into the variability of effects. In T.D. Cook et al. (Eds.), *Meta-analysis for explanation.* Beverly Hills, CA: Sage.

Lochman, J.E. (1992). Cognitive behavioral interventions with aggressive boys: Three-year follow up and prevention efforts. *Journal of Consulting and Clinical Psychology, 60,* 426–432.

Lochman, J.E., Burch, P.R., Curry, J.F., & Lampron, L.B. (1984). Treatment and generalization effects of cognitive behavioral and goal setting interventions with aggressive boys. *Journal of Consulting and Clinical Psychology, 52,* 915–916.

Long, N.J. (1992). Managing a shooting incident. *Journal of Emotional and Behavioral Problems, 1*(1), 23–25.

Lovell, R., & Pope, C.E. (1993). Recreational interventions. In A.P. Goldstein & C.R. Huff (Eds.), *The gang intervention handbook.* Champaign, IL: Research Press.

Lucker, G.W., Rosenfield, D., Sikes, J., & Aronson, E. (1976). Performance in the interdependent classroom: A field study. *American Educational Research Journal, 13,* 115–123.

Magdid, K., & McKelvey, C.A. (1987). *Children without a conscience.* New York: Bantam.

Mayers, P. (1977). *The relation between structural elements and the experience of enjoyment in high-school classes.* Unpublished manuscript, University of Chicago.

McPartland, J., & Nettles, S. (1993). Using community adults as advocates or mentors for at-risk middle school students: A two-year evaluation. In M. Freedman (Ed.), *The kindness of strangers: Adult mentors, urban youth, and the new volunteerism.* San Francisco: Jossey-Bass.

Metropolitan Life Insurance Company. (1994). *Metropolitan Life survey of the American teacher: Violence in America's public schools.* New York: Author.

Miller, J.A., & Peterson, D.W. (1987). Peer-influenced academic interventions. In C.A. Maher & J.E. Zins (Eds.), *Psychoeducational interventions in the schools.* New York: Pergamon.

Miller, W.B. (1958). Lower class culture as a generating milieu of gang delinquency. *Journal of Social Issues, 14,* 5–19.

Miller, W.B. (1974). American youth gangs: Past and present. In A. Blumberg (Ed.), *Current perspectives on human behavior.* New York: Knopf.

Moore, J.W. (1983). Isolation and stigmatization in the development of an underclass: The case of Chicano gangs in East Los Angeles. *Social Problems, 33,* 1–12.

Moore, J.W. (1991). *Going down to the barrio: Home boys and home girls in change.* Philadelphia: Temple University Press.

Moore, J.W., Vigil, D., & Garcia, R. (1983). Residence and territoriality in Chicano gangs. *Social Problems, 31,* 182–194.

Mulvihill, D.J., Tumin, M.M., & Curtis, L.A. (1969). *Crimes of violence.* Washington, DC: National Commission on the Causes and Prevention of Violence.

Mydans, S. (1991, May 7). As cultures meet gang wars paralyze a city in California. *The New York Times,* sec. A, pp. 1–5.

National Association of School Safety and Law Enforcement Officers. (1994). *NASSLEO Quarterly, 3,* 1–2.

National Center for Education Statistics. (1992). *Public school principal survey on safe, disciplined, and drug-free schools.* Washington, DC: U.S. Department of Education.

National Coalition on Television Violence. (1994, July-September). *NCTV News,* p. 2.

National League of Cities. (1994). *School violence in America's cities: NLC survey overview.* Washington, DC: Author.

National School Safety Center. (1995). *Student searches and the law: An administrator's guide to conducting searches on campus.* Malibu, CA: Pepperdine University.

Oleson v. Board of Education of School District No. 228, 676 F.Supp 820 (N.D. Ill., 1987)

Padilla, F.M. (1992). *The gang as an American enterprise.* New Brunswick, NJ: Rutgers University Press.

Prophet, M. (1990). Safe schools in Portland. *American School Board Journal, 177,* 28–30.

Remboldt, C. (1994). *Violence in schools: The enabling factor.* Minneapolis: Johnson Institute.

Revere, G.P. (1997, July 9 &10). Attacking gangs on Rez. *Tri-Valley Dispatch,* pp. 1, 18.

Rosenthal, R., & Jacobson, L. (1968). *Pygmalion in the classroom: Teacher expectations and pupils' intellectual development.* New York: Holt, Rinehart & Winston.

Rotheram, M.J. (1982). Social skills training with underachievers, disruptive and exceptional children. *Psychology in the Schools, 19,* 532–539.

Sanders, W.B. (1994). *Gangbangs and drive-bys.* New York: Aldine De Gruyter.

Scruggs, T.E., Mastropieri, M.A., & Richter, L. (1985). Peer tutoring with behaviorally disordered students: Social and academic benefits. *Behavioral Disorders, 10,* 283–294.

Sharon, S., & Sharon, Y. (1976). *Small group teaching.* Englewood Cliffs, NJ: Educational Technology.

Shereskewsky, M., & Ross, S. (1997). Community alternatives serve at-risk youth. *School Safety, 4,* 25–26.

Sherman, L.W., Gottfredson, D., MacKenzie, D., Eck, J., Reuter, P., & Bushway, S. (1997). *Preventing crime: What works, what doesn't, what's promising* (Report to the United States Congress). Baltimore: University of Maryland, Department of Criminology and Criminal Justice, Office of Justice Programs.

Siegel, L.M., & Senna, J.J. (1991). *Juvenile delinquency: Theory, practice and law.* St. Paul: West.

Slavin, R.E. (1985). An introduction to cooperative learning research. In R.E. Slavin, S. Sharan, S. Kagen, R. Hertz-Lazarowitz, C. Webb, & R. Schmuck (Eds.), *Learning to cooperate, cooperating to learn.* New York: Plenum.

Slavin, R.E. (1977). *Student learning team techniques: Narrowing the achievement gap between the races.* Baltimore: Johns Hopkins University, Center for Social Organization of Schools.

Slavin, R.E. (1978). Student teams and achievement divisions. *Journal of Research and Development in Education, 12,* 39–40.

Slavin, R.E., Leavey, M., & Madden, N.A. (1982, April). *Effects of student teams and individualized instruction on student mathematics achievement, attitudes, and behaviors.* Paper presented at the annual conference of the American Educational Research Association, New York.

Slavin, R.E., & Oickle, E. (1981). Effects of cooperative learning teams on student achievement and race relations: Treatment by race interactions. *Sociology of Education, 54,* 174–180.

Spergel, I.A. (1990). Youth gangs: Continuity and change. In M. Tonry & N. Morris (Eds.), *Crime and justice: A review of research* (Vol. 12). University of Chicago Press.

Spergel, I.A. (1995). *The youth gang problem.* New York: Oxford University Press.

Spergel, I.A. (1996, June). *The Little Village Gang Violence Reduction Project: A comprehensive and integrated approach.* Paper presented at the National Youth Gang Symposium, Dallas.

Spergel, I.A., & Curry, G.D. (1993). The National Youth Gang Survey: A research and development process. In A.P. Goldstein & C.R. Huff, *The gang intervention handbook.* Champaign, IL: Research Press.

Stanton, B., & Galbraith, J. (1994). Drug trafficking among African-American early adolescents: Prevalence, consequences, and associated behaviors and beliefs. *Pediatrics, 93,* 1039–1043.

Stephens, R.D. (1992, March). Gangs vs. schools: Assessing the score in your community. *School Safety Update* (National School Safety Center News Service), p. 8.

Stephens, R.D. (1993). School-based interventions: Safety and security. In A.P. Goldstein & C.R. Huff (Eds.), *The gang intervention handbook.* Champaign, IL: Research Press.

Stephens, R.D. (1997). National trends in school violence. In A.P. Goldstein & J.P. Conoley (Eds.), *School violence intervention: A practical handbook.* New York: Guilford.

Straus, M.A. (1994). *Beating the devil out of them.* New York: Lexington.

Thompson, D.W., & Jason, L.A. (1988). Street gangs and preventive interventions. *Criminal Justice and Behavior, 15,* 323–333.

Thrasher, F.M. (1963). *The gang.* University of Chicago Press. (Original work published 1927)

Thurman, Q.C., Giacomazzi, A.L., Reisig, M.D., & Mueller, D.G. (1996). Community-based gang prevention and intervention: An evaluation of the Neutral Zone. *Crime & Delinquency, 42,* 279–295.

Tinker v. Des Moines Independent Community School District, 393 U.S. 503 (1969)

Tobler, N.A. (1992). Drug prevention programs can work: Research findings. *Journal of Addictive Diseases, 11,* 1–28.

Trump, K.S. (1997). Security policy, personnel, and operations. In A.P. Goldstein & J.C. Conoley (Eds.), *School violence intervention: A practical handbook.* New York: Guilford.

U.S. Department of Justice. (1991). *School crime: A national crime victimization survey report.* Washington, DC: U.S. Government Printing Office.

U.S. Office of Juvenile Justice and Delinquency Prevention. (1994). *Juvenile crime, 1988–1992.* Washington, DC: Author.

U.S. Office of Juvenile Justice and Delinquency Prevention. (1995). *A comprehensive response to America's youth gang problem.* Washington, DC: Author.

U.S. Office of Juvenile Justice and Delinquency Prevention. (1997). *Communities in schools: A collaboration at work for youth.* Washington, DC: Author.

Vigil, J. (1983). Chicano gangs: One response to Mexican urban adaptation in the Los Angeles area. *Urban Anthropology, 12,* 45–75.

Vigil, J. (1990). Cholos and gangs: Culture change and street youth in Los Angeles. In C.R. Huff (Ed.), *Gangs in America.* Newbury Park, CA: Sage.

von Sternberg, B. (1997, September 18). More gang activity seen on Indian reservations, federal officials say. *Minneapolis Star Tribune,* sec. A, p. 4.

Walberg, H.J. (1985). Instructional theories and research evidence. In M.C. Wang & H.J. Walberg (Eds.), *Adapting instruction to individual differences.* Berkeley: McCutchan.

Wang, M.C. (1981). Mainstreaming exceptional children. Some instructional design and implementation considerations. *Elementary School Journal, 18,* 195–221.

Weiner, B. (1984). Principles for a theory of student motivation and their application within an attributional framework. In R. Ames & D.C. Ames (Eds.), *Research on motivation in education: Vol. 1. Student motivation.* Orlando, FL: Academic.

Werner, E.E., & Smith, R.S. (1982). *Vulnerable but invincible.* New York: McGraw-Hill.

Wilson, W.J. (1991). Studying inner city social dislocations: The challenge of public agenda research: 1990 presidential address. *American Sociological Review, 56,* 1–14.

Wise, P.S., Genshaft, J.L., & Byrley, M.B. (1987). Study-skills training: A comprehensive approach. In C.A. Maker & J.E. Zins (Eds.), *Psychoeducational interventions in the schools.* New York: Pergamon.

Youth violence. (1991, November 25). *The New York Times,* p. 23.

Youth Works. (1997). *Youth works: Volunteers with youth.* Louisville, KY: Author.

Name Index

Subject Index

About the Authors

Arnold P. Goldstein joined the clinical psychology section of Syracuse University's Psychology Department in 1963 and both taught there and directed its Psychotherapy Center until 1980. In 1981, he founded the Center for Research on Aggression. He joined Syracuse University's Division of Special Education in 1985 and in 1990 helped organize and codirect the New York State Task Force on Juvenile Gangs. He is currently Professor Emeritus of Education and Psychology. Dr. Goldstein has a career-long interest, as both researcher and practitioner, in difficult-to-reach clients. Since 1980, his main research and psychoeducational focus has been youth violence. Dr. Goldstein's many books include, among others, *The Prepare Curriculum: Teaching Prosocial Competencies, Delinquents on Delinquency, The Gang Intervention Handbook, Break It Up: A Teacher's Guide to Managing Student Aggression,* and the recently revised editions of *Skillstreaming the Adolescent: New Strategies and Perspectives for Teaching Prosocial Skills* and *Aggression Replacement Training: A Comprehensive Intervention for Aggressive Youth.*

Donald W. Kodluboy earned a doctorate in experimental psychology, emphasizing psychopharmacology and applied behavior analysis, from the University of Minnesota before moving into the field of school psychology. Practicing in the Minneapolis public schools for 22 years, he has specialized in programming for youth with severe behavior disorders. Dr. Kodluboy has observed the growth of street gangs in the Midwest for more than 12 years and is currently researching the development of street gangs among Southeast Asian youth. He is a member of the Midwest Gang Investigators Association and a past member of the St. Paul Community Development Task Force's Safety Subcommittee, the Public Safety Advisory Council for the city of St. Paul, and the Ramsey County Youth Gang Task Force. He has contributed to several texts on the topic of youth gangs and conducts identification- and intervention-focused training for educators on the critical issues facing schools and communities confronted with street gangs.